Embracing
Midlife

Congregations as Support Systems

Lynne M. Baab

Foreword by Nancy B. Millner

An Alban Institute Publication

Library of Congress Catalog Card Number 99-73546
ISBN 1-56699-216-8

CONTENTS

FOREWORD

"How can religious organizations better serve people in midlife?" I asked a delightful, faithful, and somewhat disillusioned friend. "Better than they do," she responded without hesitation. My friend, though her words may sound demanding, is correct. Lynne Baab's gently challenging book can assist congregations and other religious organizations in the noble effort of learning "to do better."

Now, my friend has some things to learn too. She needs to learn to articulate her needs to her congregation and to realize that no institution is capable of fully meeting her needs. And her congregation and leaders throughout the religious community need to learn to hear the desire and pain behind her comments rather than only demand and pressure. If these things can happen, healing and growth can occur for both people in midlife and the faith communities to which they belong. They can both be transformed. Lynne Baab's book, with her understanding and practical suggestions, makes a significant contribution to this transformation.

The first step toward healing and growth for individuals and faith communities is a bold recognition of the need for transformation. It is the nature of the midlife passage to make demands and to initiate change and growth for the sake of renewal. These inclinations can often feel like a threat to the status quo. During the middle passage the voices demanding reassessment often sound confused and questioning both to those who speak and those who hear. The voices come disguised as relationship difficulties, work dissatisfaction, anxiety, illness, vague questioning, discontent, and even spiritual crisis. The voice of midlife can be loud, intrusive, and defiant but it is more likely to be soft, evasive, and sad. It is most often a voice that simply becomes less and less audible as it moves from the front row of the institution to the back row on its way toward an unobtrusive, and often final, exit.

Lynne Baab assists us to recognize these midlife voices as she offers delightful, realistic stories from people in their middle years telling of their disappointments and their losses.

Important as it is for congregations, religious leaders, and individuals to recognize when the middle passage is occurring, this recognition is not enough. It is also necessary to understand the nature of midlife dynamics as well as the prevalent fear and distrust of these dynamics. Discontent, confusion, ambiguity, changing behavior, hard questions without apparent answers, and people's turning their attention toward self-exploration rather than institutional tasks are typical of the middle passage. These dynamics are not always understood or welcomed. Congregations and their leaders, feeling defensive and fearful, sometimes label people experiencing the middle passage as malcontents, selfish, or even unfaithful.

Baab helps normalize and therefore lessen the fear we might experience by educating us about midlife dynamics. Her book reduces anxiety in congregations that fear they don't know how to react as she shows ways to explore and respond to midlife issues of loss, difficult relationships, anger, fear, sexuality, paradox and tension, pain, and changing relationship to God. She helps readers learn how to be present with people in midlife transition without feeling that they will be engulfed or that they must solve all midlife problems. In fact, I would think it might come as a great relief to realize that midlife issues are rarely solved but rather are almost always outgrown. The most loving congregations and most conscientious ministers and rabbis need not feel that they must bear the responsibility to fix midlife challenges, but they do need to learn how to be responsive to people in midlife transition. If they are not responsive, people in midlife—particularly those who have given much to their congregations—will rightly feel deserted. They will feel that their faith communities have abandoned them just when their need was greatest.

The good news is that congregations and individuals can both benefit by responding to the change and growth demanded. Successful midlife transition calls individuals and institutions to adulthood and adult spirituality beyond organizational structure, sacred word, and ritual to personal relationship and personal commitment to God. The transformation delivers from superficiality, stagnation, complacency, and rigidity and offers the possibility for renewal, creativity, and fullness of life. Successful midlife transition leads to more personal authenticity, more committed contribution on behalf of others, and true community that can embrace and appreciate differences.

With her compassion and knowledge of midlife experience, congregational life, and Jung's typology, Baab offers readers specific, practical suggestions for their own authentic spiritual growth and for true spiritual community that can accept and appreciate God-given differences.

We can agree with the woman mentioned earlier that religious institutions can "do better than they do," and with Baab's help we can promise
her that, in fact, many congregations will.

Nancy Bost Millner

PREFACE

Methodist minister Thad Rutter[1] believes that we have two primary vo-
cabularies in congregations. One vocabulary comes from the language of
the mechanics of congregational life: the budget, the building, committees,
and boards. The second vocabulary comes from the language of theological
truth: right and wrong, interpretation of Scripture, and questions of ethical
behavior.

Rutter argues that we need to add a third vocabulary, that of relationship and connection with God and emotions before God. I heard the longing
for this third vocabulary when I interviewed people about their midlife experiences.

This book is written for Christians, Unitarians, and Jews who want
their congregations to be a place of support and welcome for people in the
midlife years, the years between 35 and 55. Even though Christians, Unitarians, and Jews have very different faith priorities and vocabulary in some
areas, the issues that come up at midlife are remarkably similar.

Midlife can be a time of questioning: Who am I? Why am I here? What
is my purpose in life? How can and should I impact the world around me? If
I died tomorrow, what would be unfinished?

These questions tap into deeper faith questions: Where is God in my
life? Am I truly alone or is God there? Does God care for me? Why have I
experienced God so little in the first half of life? Why has God not answered
so many of my prayers? Why doesn't God make life easier?

And there is one more question: How can I experience connection
with God more fully?

One woman who directs a retreat center says that people at midlife
who come for retreats seem to have little interest in obtaining more information about anything. They come needing time to process and reexamine

what they already know. They want to examine their lives and look for God's footprint, God's hand, God's presence.

People at midlife are often not primarily interested in the language of church structures, although they may be quite competent at working within committees and task forces. They are usually not primarily interested in theological truth, although they may enjoy theological study or discussions about ethics. From my interviews, it seems that first and foremost they long for connection with God, and they want to be sure their lives have meaning. They long to see their congregations develop this third vocabulary, the language of emotive connection and heartfelt relationship with the transcendent.

This presents a tremendous opportunity for congregations. Yet many congregations have done a pretty thorough job of ignoring midlife. Is that because midlife is often a time of questions, and questions can be threatening? Is it because at midlife many people move towards ambiguity, and most congregations prefer black and white answers? Or is it because we lack that third vocabulary that Thad Rutter describes, and we are simply not comfortable discussing emotive connection with God?

Maybe churches ignore the issues of midlife because we believe that by the age of 35 or 40, people finally "have it all together." They aren't falling apart and they aren't experiencing serious needs; therefore, they don't really need attention.

Is Midlife Angst Real?

In February 1999 the MacArthur Foundation released the results of a ten-year study that surveyed more than 3,000 Americans between the ages of 25 and 74. The study found that people between the ages of 40 and 60 had a greater sense of well-being in general than at any other time in life. When my local newspaper, the *Seattle Times*, reported on this research, the front-page headline screamed, "Midlife Crisis a Myth."

The study found that only about 10 percent of both men and women experienced the existential upheaval we often call a "midlife crisis." That figure is consistent with the conversations and interviews that form the foundation for this book. Only a handful of the people I talked with used the language of "midlife crisis."

Many others I interviewed talked about the real-life issues they have encountered between 35 and 55. Their parents are ill or dying. They have experienced the agony of infertility. Their children are rebellious teenagers. They long to be married and have a family, but they are still single at 45. They are bored with their jobs. They don't have a job. They are unhappy in their marriages.

These issues do not necessarily dominate their lives, so if they had been participants in the MacArthur Foundation study, they might have reported general well-being. But these real-life circumstances still raise questions. People who are involved in faith communities look to their faith for answers. Are we prepared to be the kind of congregations that provide support for the various kinds of midlife transitions? Do we want to continue to limit ourselves to the traditional focus in our programs: ministry to children, youth, young adults, seniors, and those in need outside the congregation?

Midlife Averages

Maybe we have ignored midlife in our congregations because we believe that good, faithful people won't struggle, or because we don't have a language for personal intimacy with God, or because we think people at midlife are mostly doing fine. Maybe we have ignored it because it is hard to make generalizations about it. Whatever the reason, I'm convinced we can do a better job caring for the people in our congregations between the ages of 35 and 55.

I met Jenn in the new members' class at my church. Soon after I met her, she told me her younger brother had committed suicide at 16, only a few months before.

Several months later, just as I was finishing this book, Jenn and I were riding home from a women's retreat. In the car she reflected on her brother's death. She told me she had been dealing with death almost all her life. Her father died when she was nine, and in her mid-teens her favorite aunt died the same year as her grandfather.

"I've had so many losses," she said. "I've learned to live each day for what it offers. All we have is the present. Another loss might be around the corner. I experience so much joy and happiness when good things happen, more than my friends do. That's how all these deaths have shaped me."

Jenn, in her mid-20s, sounds like someone in her 40s or 50s who has learned to accept the reality that life is full of loss and that all we have is this precious moment. The conversation with Jenn made clear to me that when we discuss midlife, to a large extent we are talking about averages. Most people will be in their 40s before they experience the number of devastating losses that Jenn has faced. Most people will be in their 40s or even 50s before they learn the positive lessons that loss brings: the ability to experience joy in the present moment and to feel intense gratitude for the gift of life.

Some people will learn those lessons early, like Jenn has. Some people will learn those lessons in their 60s or 70s. Some people will never learn them. But the largest number of people will learn them during their midlife years.

More people will face the confusion of parenting adolescents during the midlife years than at any other time. Certainly some people in their 30s will be parents of adolescents, and in the years to come many more people in their 60s will be coping with adolescent children. But most of us who have children will be between 35 and 55 when we find ourselves baffled and confused by all sorts of emotions triggered by living with adolescents.

More people will face the difficulties of aging parents during the midlife years than at any other time. Certainly, some people like Jenn will lose parents when they are children, or they may be like my mother and my father who were in their 60s when their mothers died. But it is during the midlife years, more than at any other age, that many people will experience their parents' ill health and deaths.

People face challenging personal transitions throughout their lives, such as career change, divorce, and cross-country moves. Some of these transitions trigger questions about the purpose of our lives. Some of these transitions motivate us to make significant changes in the direction of our lives.

One person might find himself asking soul-searching questions after a divorce at age 28, and someone else at 60 might find herself questioning the meaning of life after the death of her grown child. These life-changing transitions with the attendant questions about life can happen at any age, but a lot of them seem to happen in the midlife years.

Maybe this is part of the reason why congregations have ignored midlife and its issues. Maybe it is simply very difficult to pin down.

Therefore we can never say, "At midlife you will experience this or that." But what we can say is that *often* midlife is characterized by facing significant questions and learning to cope with losses.

I'm convinced that congregations will be healthier if their leaders become aware of the common issues and transitions faced by people in that age group, even if not everyone in that age group is facing them. I'm convinced of the richness of questions and the benefits of growth that come from facing losses in community rather than alone. I'm convinced that our congregations will be healthier if we encourage an atmosphere of experimentation and creativity in spirituality.

As I write these words in 1999, the front edge of the baby boom generation is close to the end of the midlife years, and the youngest boomers have just entered midlife. This generation is the most psychologically sophisticated generation that has ever passed through congregations. They read and hear about the issues concerning midlife in the secular press. Generation X (those born between 1965 and about 1978) will be next, and they are even more psychologically sophisticated than the baby boomers. Congregations cannot afford to continue to ignore midlife as these two generations move along in age. Besides, midlife offers a tremendous opportunity to help people develop their own personal vocabulary to connect with God. Why pass up such a wonderful opportunity?

The Sources for This Book

This book began with a slip of paper with these words written on it: "You must think it's weird that I would get to this place in my life and not know what I want to do."

The speaker was an old friend of mine, whom I have called "Rebecca" in chapter 1. At that time she was 40. She had spent the previous decade raising children and dealing with illness. She didn't know what she wanted to do next, and she was ashamed of her indecision. When we were talking on the phone that day, I was so struck by her comment that I wrote it down on a slip of paper. When I found the slip of paper on my desk a few weeks later, I got out a file folder, labeled it "Midlife," and threw the scrap of paper into it.

I continued to collect thoughts and observations about midlife from other conversations. When I began working on this book in earnest, I began scheduling interviews. All told, this book is based on interviews with more than 40 people in Christian, Jewish, and Unitarian congregations, and informal conversations with dozens more.

This book is also based on a wide variety of books on midlife and other related topics. My goal is to present the issues of midlife and a range of voices about midlife, with practical suggestions for the ways congregations can respond.

When you hear the voices and stories of people at midlife recounted here, you should know that all the names of the people I interviewed have been changed, along with some of the identifying details. In a few cases the stories are composites.

I have chosen to define the midlife years as the age span from 35 to 55 because we usually use "young adult" to describe people in their 20s and early 30s. The U.S. government recently defined 55 as the beginning of "senior adulthood." So that leaves a group of people in the middle—between young adults and seniors.

A Word about Journaling

At the end of each chapter you will find questions for reflection. The first set of questions is designed to be used by individuals reading this book. The questions can be used for reflection or journaling. The questions can also be used for group discussion.

The second set of questions at the end of each chapter is designed to be used by congregational leaders and clergy who want to make their congregations more midlife friendly.

I want to encourage you to journal as you respond to the questions for individuals. Several recent studies indicate the remarkable healing power in getting our thoughts and our emotions into words on paper.[2] One study recommends writing about disturbing experiences for 15 to 20 minutes a day for three or four days in a row. The instructions suggest that people not try to be polished writers; just try to be honest about what you are feeling. One study, described in the *Journal of the American Medical Association*, showed that such writing exercises can actually reduce asthma and rheumatoid arthritis! Our goal here is to move through the losses and stresses of midlife in a healthy manner. If writing down emotions can help reduce asthma, surely writing about what we are feeling can bring health and healing with regard to midlife issues.

A Wish for God's Blessings

If you are at midlife yourself, I wish you joy and peace in the journey. I hope you will meet God in new ways and grow in depth and wisdom as you move through midlife. I hope that the stories recounted here will be encouraging, and that you will have a very rich time exploring new patterns of spirituality and service during your midlife years.

If you are reading this book primarily to benefit your congregation, I wish you God's blessing as you endeavor to act on some of the suggestions presented here. I know we can do a better job helping congregation members between 35 and 55 to grow, flourish, and bear fruit.

ACKNOWLEDGMENTS

I could not have written this book without the dozens of people who were willing to talk with me about their midlife experiences. They gave me wonderful insights about midlife and lots of ideas for the ways congregations can help their members navigate the midlife years.

My heartfelt thanks go to everyone who talked to me about midlife. Some were brief conversations, some were extended interviews, some were in group settings, and I'm grateful for them all. My particular thanks go to Jack and Helen Akamine, Steven Albright, Joleen Burgess, Linda Bylsma, Sherry Campbell, Charlotte and John Clark-Mahoney, Bruce Davis, Jay Derr, Rev. Kathleen Everett, Rabbi Dov Gartenberg, Gary Glenney, Rev. Sandy Hackett, Linda Harmony, Rev. William Houff, Peter Ilgenfritz, Marilyn Israel, Barry Johns, Rev. Mark Labberton, Linda Lambert, Ann Marmesh, Rev. Kathleen McTigue, Rev. Kent McCulloch, John Morford, Jeff Parrish, Mary Patrick, Amory Peck, Sharon Peterson, Susan Phillips, Golda Posey, Mike Purdy, Marsha Rhodes, Nancy Ross, Gordon Sako, Tina Sellers, Bob Schultz, Rev. Marie Sheldon, Ben Sherman, Sherwin Shinn, Rabbi Jonathan Singer, Kim Smith, Jeff and Margie Van Duzer, and Jo Kelley Welsh.

To Rev. Boyd Stockdale and Rabbi James Mirel I want to express my thanks for their helpful ideas about midlife and their encouragement about the manuscript. I also want to thank the people who read my manuscript so carefully and gave me so many valuable suggestions: Rene Doran, Beth Hess, Susan Snyder, and Fred Wagner. My Alban Institute editor, Beth Ann Gaede, was wonderfully supportive and encouraging in the midst of giving me constructive and helpful feedback. Most of all I want to thank my husband, Dave—my partner in the midlife journey.

CHAPTER 1

Introduction to Midlife

I considered all that my hands had done and the toil I had spent in doing it, and again, all was vanity and a chasing after wind, and there was nothing to be gained under the sun.

Ecclesiastes 2:11

Will is 52. He remembers distinctly what happened 10 years ago. He began to experience intense anger. He felt as if he had been lied to by the church and by his parents and teachers. The middle-class values of materialism, he began to believe, were simply wrong. He felt that the real questions—questions of eternal values—were never discussed in school, in church, or at home.

"When's the last time you heard a sermon on preparing for death?" Will asks. "In my early 40s, I was peeping over the hill looking at my own death, and no one seemed to care. I was looking for answers and no one seemed to have them. Most of the questions came from a sense of my own mortality. The picture is a whole lot larger than you ever thought, and you realize that if you can't understand it, you're doomed.

"My anger was caused by my disappointment in myself and in the forces I had initially seen as benevolent, which I felt had betrayed me. I found myself thinking, 'If this is all life is, if this is what it means, I might as well go ahead and do something destructive.'

"I know that most people don't have a reaction like this, but it was very intense for me."

Eventually Will and his wife sold their house in a large city. With the proceeds, they were able to buy 17 acres in Montana, where they now live a very simple life. Will had been a Protestant churchgoer for much of his life, but after the move to Montana, he began to find in the Roman Catholic Church the answers he was seeking. He is deeply committed now both to Catholicism and to living off the land as much as possible.

Rebecca, a 40-year-old mother of four, illustrates another face of midlife. She survived cancer in her mid-30s. Two of her children had severe health problems as preschoolers. As the children have entered into late elementary school and middle school, and as everyone's heath has improved, Rebecca, for the first time in a decade, has a small amount of time to spare. She finds herself asking a lot of questions.

"What am I going to do with the rest of my life?" Rebecca asks. "All the other women I know from the synagogue either have fast-paced and fascinating careers, or they seem to be perfectly content to stay at home with their children. The career women make me feel like I've been left behind, and the homemakers make me feel guilty. Why isn't it enough to take care of my children? Why can't I be content with this important role in life? Why do I want more? And how in the world do I decide what to do next? You must think it's weird that I would get to this place in my life and not know what I want to do."

In contrast to Rebecca, Fitz is content with his life. In his early 40s, he is happily married, enjoys his son and daughter very much, and experiences contentment in his work.

Fitz, a lifelong church attender, remembers back to his college years when he was very intense about his faith. He remembers exciting retreats, fascinating books, and conversations long into the night about the meaning of life and the significance of the Christian faith.

"Midlife Christianity, more than anything else, is in danger of complacency," he reflects. "The church has a tendency to assume for folks like us that we're fine and there's no need for us to grow any more. And it's true that I don't feel a need to dive into deep theological questions. I have a confidence that God is there. My spiritual life isn't like a roller coaster, as it was when I was younger. I no longer fear losing God.

"On the one hand there is this knowledge and confidence in my faith, but on the other hand there is also much less discovery and recognition of God's presence in each moment. There is less vividness, fewer emotions, fewer highs. I already know the major stories in the Bible, so I have less of a sense of discovery and less hunger to read the Bible. I have to say there's almost a numbness about all of my life, including my faith.

"The question is how to restore freshness to faith without returning to the roller coaster of youth."

Midlife

In Will, Rebecca, and Fitz we hear three voices of midlife. Will's anger and desire to reframe the priorities of his life are common at this life stage, as is Rebecca's confusion about what to do with the rest of her life. Fitz experiences both contentment and flatness, another frequent experience at midlife.

For many years people viewed adulthood as a flat plain, a straight path across a level field after the tumult of adolescence and before the decline of old age. Now we are beginning to understand that the path is not straight; there are predictable turns and changes in the path. Nor is the field level. Many of us will encounter totally unexpected events that can change and shape us dramatically. Divorce, death in the family, unplanned career changes, life-threatening illnesses, and many other events cause ups and downs on the journey through adulthood.

During the midlife years, some people experience a major transition that causes them to change the direction of their lives in a significant way. Some might use the language of "midlife crisis" to describe such a transition. Others do not experience major changes in their lives during the midlife years, but many do notice subtle shifts in the way they think about things.

Some of these shifts and transitions seem to originate inside ourselves. For some of us, life stays the same on the outside, but we find ourselves wondering about the purpose of our lives. We don't really want to live the second half of our lives the same way we lived the first half. We find ourselves asking questions. We may find ourselves asking a lot of questions, some of them touching on issues deep inside us.

Some midlife transitions and shifts originate in external events. The children become adolescents or leave home. We lose our job, or our spouse decides not to stay married. We have a major change in health. Any life event can precipitate changes in us that go far beyond the event that triggered the change.

Social scientists are divided on the subject of midlife. Some of them believe that the midlife transition has significance far beyond other life transitions. Others are more interested in the pattern of transitions across the human life span. They note that most people experience a transition every seven to ten years, and any of them can trigger significant changes in the way we live.

Even if we agree that most adults face transitions every seven to ten years, the transitions that occur between 35 and 55 still have particular weight. In part, these transitions are difficult to face because of the myriad responsibilities that most people in this age group have, such as mortgages, children approaching the need for college tuition, and aging parents. In addition, biological forces are at work in women in this age group as they face menopause and the loss of fertility. Both men and women in this age range are usually experiencing a decline in physical strength and agility. Because of the death of parents and increased personal health problems, both of which are common in this age group, facing one's mortality is a common experience.

Psychologists Eleanor Corlett and Nancy Millner are among those who acknowledge the many transitions of adult life but also believe that midlife often involves deep issues and significant questions. They write, "Successful midlife transition has at its core elements that distinguish it from all other life transitions—the search for one's authentic self and one's unique mission and purpose."[1]

We've lived a couple of decades of adult life, and something inside us calls us to reevaluation and reexamination. We make midcourse corrections. We ask questions, some of them quite uncomfortable. We face the fact that some of our dreams will never be achieved. We reframe other dreams and begin to take steps to achieve them. We prepare to enter the second half of life.

Carl Jung wrote about midlife many decades ago. The patterns of behavior, he believed, that worked in the morning of life would no longer be effective in life's afternoon. Changes would be necessary, and the task of midlife is to evaluate one's life in order to be able to make those changes.

Retreat director Joyce Rupp writes, "Midlife is a turning point, a time when one can no longer go by the dreams and life-approach of one's youth. To simply continue the way one has from youth onward can mean death for one's ability to grow. Midlife is an opportunity to turn toward greater life or wholeness."[2]

By and large, congregations ignore the significance of this life stage. Certainly, in our communities of faith, we embrace the concept of enabling our members to "turn toward greater life or wholeness." But we often don't understand what is happening in the midlife years, so we lose an opportunity to come alongside members in this life stage. In congregations we often ignore the importance of asking questions, and questions are essential to this stage of life. We desire order and harmony in our congregations. Yet midlife can be a time of tumult and disorder, and it requires an act of conscious commitment for a congregation to embrace even a small portion of the chaos of midlife.

At a church dinner I overheard someone saying, "I hate the term 'midlife crisis.' It's always used as an excuse. 'He left his wife because of his midlife crisis,' or 'He started an affair because of his midlife crisis.' I don't have much patience with this midlife crisis stuff, because having an affair is wrong, no matter which way you look at it."

In this book we will look at the life events that often occur between the ages of 35 and 55. We will explore the kinds of questions that are triggered by those events, along with the questions that seem to appear out of nowhere for some people in that age group. We will consider the ways that congregations can come alongside people in the wide variety of situations that are common in the midlife years.

My hope is that this book will help people avoid the kind of midlife crisis that involves affairs and broken marriages. I agree with Mike, an Episcopal minister, who said, "Train wrecks at midlife are not required. At midlife, we're making the transition into old age, which is not easy. But it's not necessary to crash if we're conscious and aware of the pitfalls."

My Own Midlife Story

I experienced a significant midlife transition that began when I was 38 and lasted until I was 45. It wasn't particularly intense for all that time, but looking back, I can see major changes happening in the way I viewed myself and in my choices for my life.

I finished my seminary degree in 1990 when I was 38. I had been attending seminary part-time for 10 years while I stayed home with my children. When I graduated, my sons were eight and 10 years old, growing in independence. In May 1990, right before seminary graduation, I got a job editing a denominational publication. In the fall I got another editing job, and I began teaching as an adjunct faculty member in the religion department of a local university.

I hadn't worked for pay since before I had children. I took great joy in each paycheck. Even more important, I thrived on the work. The teaching was easy because I'd been teaching adult classes in churches for years. But it felt great to be paid to teach. The editing jobs were wonderfully challenging. I had to learn many new skills: how to negotiate and work with the press that published the papers, how to use desktop publishing software to do layout, and how to conduct efficient phone interviews for articles. I began to regain a view of myself as competent and intelligent.

I had battled depression throughout the decade of the 1980s, and, surprisingly, this newfound joy in work didn't do anything to relieve the depression. But now the depression had a voice, the voice of regret. Why had I never considered going to graduate school right after college, when I could have studied full time and then embraced a career? Why had I never really considered a career at all in my focus on having children? Why had I stayed home with my kids for 10 years, instead of stepping out into the work world? Even more importantly, how had I lost my way so profoundly as a young mother? I had forgotten I was a competent and intelligent person.

The questions went deeper. The depression I had experienced as a young mother had led me into a powerful kind of self-loathing. What was wrong with me that I found it so difficult to focus my life solely around my children? Why couldn't I be content as a homemaker? And why had I wasted all those years hating myself, overeating for comfort, and feeling worthless?

And then there were the questions about God. Where had God been throughout all the depression? Why had God allowed me to make such bad choices in my life? Why hadn't God helped me? Where was God in the midst of all my negative emotions?

In 1992 I qualified for a depression research project in which I was given 20 free sessions of cognitive therapy. The therapist worked with me to tease out the beliefs that lay beneath my depression. I accessed these beliefs through a series of questions: What kind of a person would struggle so much with being a mother? What kind of a person would be overweight? What kind of a person would have an untidy house?

These questions had been floating around my brain for years, but I had never taken the time to answer them. The therapist forced me to provide answers, and the answer was always the same: only a terrible, horrible, awful person would struggle as a mother, overeat, and be untidy. As I exposed this answer and the belief that lay behind the answer—that struggling, untidy, and overweight people are worthless—I began to realize I'd been living my life by values that I simply don't believe. In the light of God's grace, it simply cannot be true that struggling, untidy, and overweight people are worthless; why did I live my life as if I believed it?

Even though I began to understand the power of this warped belief system inside me, I was unable to shake it off. My depression lifted a little, but I still kept falling into the trap of self-loathing.

My midlife transition came to a major turning point in 1994 when I got an obscure lung disease. I gasped for breath for six frustrating weeks before the doctors came up with an accurate diagnosis. During the sixth week I misunderstood something the doctor said, and I spent a week believing I was going to die. This is an experience I recommend to everyone! It clarified so many things. During that week, and in the months of recovery that followed, the truths that were revealed in the cognitive therapy sessions were driven home. I saw clearly that I wanted to live a life more in harmony with what I really believe.

I wasn't afraid to die. This confirmed to me that my faith was real and that I firmly believed in the existence of heaven. But at the same time, I discovered I wasn't ready to die. I saw clearly that my younger son still needed me very much, and I knew I had unfinished tasks I wanted to complete.

The healing process was very slow because of the side effects of the drugs used to treat the disease. I didn't feel well for more than a year. When I got my strength back 15 months after I had gotten sick, I found I was no longer depressed. I have experienced very little depression for four years now. Being free from depression felt, and still feels, like a miracle.

The absence of depression didn't mean the midlife transition was over. I still had huge regrets about the "wasted" years of my 20s and 30s. I continued to edit two publications, but together they added up to only 15 hours a week, and I was getting bored with them. I had stopped working as an adjunct faculty because of scheduling issues. What was I going to do with the rest of my life?

I had been a candidate for ordination as a Presbyterian minister since 1990, but I never felt right about applying for pastoral jobs because they were almost all full time and I knew I needed and wanted to devote a significant amount of time to writing. I had begun to write fiction around 1990 (a manifestation of midlife creativity!), and I had no idea where that would lead.

I continued to feel very sad that I hadn't gone to graduate school right after college to get a Ph.D. so that I could be deep into a satisfying career by the time I was in my 40s. I continued to feel that I had wasted my 20s and 30s, and I felt hopeless that I would ever be able to compensate for the loss.

Sometime in 1996 I made a crucial decision. I don't know how I came to this turning point, but maybe I simply got bored with the weight of the regrets. I quit my two editing jobs that year, and I made a critical assessment of the skills I had developed over my 44 years. I observed that I could write and that I knew and understood Christian ministry. Those were my two greatest strengths and areas of competence. It would be wisest, I came to believe, to build on what I already knew and try to move forward.

Once that internal transition was accomplished, things fell into place rapidly. I was able to be ordained as a half-time Presbyterian minister in a congregation, and I got my first book contract. I still occasionally experience moments of regret about my choices in my 20s and 30s, but I see much more clearly why I made the choices I made, and I understand some of the benefits that my family and I have reaped because of those choices.

Life feels rich and wonderfully challenging. I love writing books. I am deeply moved by the privilege of being a pastor. I am humbled by being so intimately involved with the deep spiritual issues in people's lives. I minister in a vibrant and somewhat chaotic congregation, so my administrative gifts are welcomed and sorely needed. I love my husband dearly and my sons are growing into fine young men. I certainly experience stresses, irritations, difficult situations, and moments of great sadness, but all of these feel like challenges I can face with courage. They are not overwhelming obstacles.

Yet I am not finished with the midlife years. My husband and I are just at the cusp of the empty nest. We wonder what new challenges and delights lie before us. During the last few years I have experienced the deaths of a very close friend and both of my husband's parents. I know there will be many more deaths during my lifetime; some of them will surely come while I am in my midlife years. The transition I experienced between age 38 and 45—moving from being a stay-at-home mom, part-time seminary student, and church volunteer to being a pastor and writer—was surely one of the most significant transitions I will ever face. But there will be many more transitions in my life, and some of them will probably be confusing and difficult.

I watch my friends and congregation members who are still in the throes of a midlife transition. I listen to their questions about what they want to do with the rest of their lives. I watch them struggle with family issues. I long for them to be finished with this life stage, so full of questions and angst. I long for them to experience the peace of having a clearer picture of their purpose in life.

Certainly, for many people, painful family and career issues remain after midlife, but there is something about getting in touch with our values and priorities that helps us reframe our lives and move forward with more joy.

Biological Changes for Women at Midlife

You might have noticed something odd about my midlife story. I did not mention menopause. In my case, I began to experience the symptoms of perimenopause, the initial stages of menopause, just as my midlife transition was ending. These symptoms can include hot flashes, migraine headaches, changes in the menstrual cycle, and mood swings. To me, perimenopause feels like an irritating series of symptoms, but there is no particular meaning attached to it for me. However, for some women, the questions and turmoil of the midlife transition coincide with the symptoms of perimenopause. It can be difficult to separate out the physiological issues related to menopause from the psychological and spiritual issues that are happening at the same time.

Lydia was 41 when her younger child, a sensitive and artistic son, began elementary school. This event was a huge loss for Lydia because she had so greatly enjoyed staying home with her children. She loved those toddler and preschool years, the leisurely mornings of cooking pancakes with her kids, the long afternoons to do art projects or read stories out loud.

Lydia certainly wants the best for her children and rejoices at each new accomplishment. At the same time, she felt sad when her son learned to read competently and no longer wanted Lydia to read out loud to him. Her son made many new friends at school and wanted to spend a lot of time playing with those new friends, just as Lydia's daughter had when she began school. Lydia could see her children growing away from her. This felt like another loss.

Lydia and her husband had talked for many years about the fact that Lydia would need to make some career decisions after the kids started school. Lydia needs to make a financial contribution towards the kids' college tuition and towards retirement. Yet Lydia has no desire to go back to work. For her, the perfect job is raising children. As her son finished first grade and entered second grade, Lydia knew the time was coming to begin to consider career issues. Just thinking about working made Lydia feel depressed.

Lydia began to notice the symptoms of perimenopause around the same time as her son started school. Lydia experienced hot flashes that woke her up several times a night. As the months passed, Lydia became more and more tired. The hot flashes were waking her up, and she often had a hard time getting back to sleep. The sadness she was experiencing because of her children's growing independence also made her feel low and listless.

One therapist who works with many midlife women recommends that women look carefully at all the symptoms they experience during perimenopause. Some symptoms may require medical attention. In Lydia's case, she may want to talk with her doctor about hormone replacement therapy to reduce the hot flashes so she can get more sleep.

Other symptoms associated with midlife and perimenopause, such as losses and sadness, are better discussed with a therapist, a spiritual director, a pastor, or even a close friend. In Lydia's case, it would be easy to believe that her listlessness and lack of energy should be addressed medically, perhaps by the prescription of an antidepressant. That choice, however, might rob Lydia of the opportunity to grieve appropriately for the loss she is experiencing as her role as full-time mother comes to an end, and it might prevent her from facing honestly her reluctance to enter the working world.

Our culture so often encourages us to cover up our sadness, to get finished with it rapidly. Yet this denial of sadness just pushes it down inside us, letting it rest there until it comes out some other time. As we will see in chapter 3, for people who are parents, the midlife journey usually involves letting go of the roles and relationships associated with being a mother or a father. Most parents experience that loss when their children reach adolescence or leave home. Lydia is experiencing loss around parenting roles earlier. The loss is real, and all losses involve a period of grief and sadness.

What about Men's Biology at Midlife?

More writers are acknowledging the major changes men experience at midlife. These changes are not hormonal in the same way that women's are, but there are significant physical changes going on for men in their 40s and early 50s.

First and foremost, men experience a loss of physical strength. "I could always count on my body," says Ted, 52. "My body was always there for me. Now I don't sleep as well, I experience fatigue much more easily, and if I do some kind of sport for the first time in a while, I feel stiff and sore afterwards. And I'm simply not as good at tennis as I used to be. I hate this aspect of aging. I truly hate it. It makes me feel incompetent."

Noah, 48, was feeling despairing about his declining athletic abilities. No matter how much he worked out, he couldn't keep up with the younger guys at the gym. He had always relied on his body and had enjoyed the feeling of competence that his strength gave him. One day at the synagogue, he found himself expressing some of these thoughts to his rabbi, who responded by describing the Jewish tradition of valuing old age for the wisdom and opportunities it brings. "It's a time to think about how you can make an impact in the world," the rabbi said. "You won't need to work as hard to develop your career, so you can now think about the ways you can participate in *tikkun olam*, repair of the world. There will be many good deeds you will be able to do. You'll find them very satisfying."

Idea for congregations:
In your newsletters, sermons, and classes, present a positive view of aging. Describe the opportunities for service that are available for seniors, and highlight older people in your congregation who are participating in interesting service and mission programs.

Those feelings of incompetence for men can also arise at work, and somehow they can feel connected to the loss of physical strength. Ted remembers his father's frequent tirades about the younger men at work, how they had a better education than he had, how they advanced more quickly than he did. Ted carefully got a good education so he would never experience the same frustration that his father described so often. Yet in his late 40s Ted began to notice younger people, now both men and women, who seemed to be thriving in their careers, doing better than Ted ever did, advancing much more rapidly than Ted did.

Some men at midlife hate their hair, which can seem like a symbol for all this loss and fear they are experiencing. As their hair grays or falls out, it seems to represent all the losses over which we have no control.

Gail Sheehy, author of several books on life stages, has coined the term "MANopause" to describe the severe crisis that can derail men in their 50s and 60s.[3] Sheehy recommends that men in their 40s spend more effort nurturing relationships, having sincere conversations with family members and friends. She also suggests that men explore their dreams and passions, trying to rediscover the dreams they had earlier in life. Taking up a musical instrument, coaching a long-forgotten sport, or learning a hands-on craft or skill can help men access some of the parts of themselves that have been forgotten.[4]

Sheehy writes that the greatest fear for men is loss of sexual potency.[5] That fear, she believes, is realized most often in men who have not been developing themselves as whole people. That's why she recommends cultivating relationships and nurturing dreams. Women must go through menopause, Sheehy writes, but men do not have to face the pain of MANopause. It can be avoided, she believes, by preemptive attention to relationships, creative outlets, and forgotten dreams.

The Male-Female Flip-Flop

Several writers, including Sheehy,[6] describe the ways men and women seem to switch concerns and passions at midlife. After 20 years of focusing on career, many men begin to long for deepening relationships. After 20 years of nurturing children, many women find themselves exploring issues of competence and mastery.

Men may find themselves becoming more tenderhearted. One man in his 40s began to get tears in his eyes at movies for the first time in his life. The phrase "getting in touch with your feelings" may have meaning for the first time. Men may find themselves longing for deeper, more intimate connections with their wives, their children, their siblings, and/or their friends.

In addition, men may find they are tired of acting like the Rock of Gibraltar at all times. They may long for a place to be free to express their feelings of weakness, dependence, and confusion.

As these feelings emerge for men, they may wonder if something is wrong with them. If they feel trapped in their strong, silent role, they may experience depression. Embracing these changes by learning to connect with people more deeply can bring about increased zest and joy in living, along with better relationships with family and friends than ever before existed.

Women at midlife may find themselves becoming more assertive and more willing to speak their minds. If they have spent a lot of their energy for many years on mothering, their children's growing independence will free up a lot of energy for new and interesting projects. By the end of the midlife years, they may find themselves established in an exciting and totally unexpected career. They may find in themselves surprising strengths and areas of competence.

After a lifetime of full-time work, Don, 52, recently cut back to three-quarters time. Because his children have left the nest and because of his increased free time, he joined the Mitzvah Corps in his synagogue. With the other members of the corps, he prepares and delivers meals to people who have just come home from the hospital and drives seniors while they run errands. Don has been surprised at how much he enjoys this form of service. Recently a colleague's wife was in a serious accident, and Don prepared several large casseroles for the family.

Idea for congregations:
Make a way for men at midlife to serve in roles that have often been filled by women: cooking for congregational events, preparing food for people in need, and other caring ministries.

Even some women who have not had children or who have never married can experience some of these same changes. After they finish mourning the loss of the possibility of being a mother, they often find great joy in competence and achievement.

This male-female flip-flop is healthy and wonderful. This growth and change enables both men and women to become more rounded human beings, closer to what God created them to be. Yet these changes can cause problems in marriages, as the woman grows in independence and competence right at the same time as the man is longing for a more intimate relationship. Couples need to talk about the ways this pattern is emerging for them and brainstorm compromises that affirm both individuals' need for intimacy and mastery.

Metaphors for Midlife

The literature about midlife is full of vivid metaphors that can help us understand what's happening. Gail Sheehy, in *New Passages: Mapping Your
Life Across Time*, uses the analogy of the lobster, which sheds its shell at
each stage of growth. Each time the lobster gets bigger, Sheehy writes, "the
confining shell must be sloughed off, and it is left unprotected until a new
covering grows. We, too, in each passage from one stage of human growth
to the next, must shed a protective structure. We, too, are left exposed and
vulnerable—but also yeasty and embryonic again."[7] It is at these points,
she believes, that we have a heightened potential for making significant
changes in our lives that will enable us to grow.

Anne Morrow Lindbergh, in *Gift from the Sea*, writes, "Perhaps middle
age is, or should be, a period of shedding shells: the shell of ambition, the
shell of material accumulations and possessions, the shell of the ego." Perhaps, in addition, she muses, one may find the ability to shed "one's pride,
one's false ambitions, one's mask, one's armor. . . . Perhaps one can at last
in middle age, if not earlier, be completely oneself. And what a liberation
that would be!"[8]

People who are conscious of significant changes they've made at midlife
will probably enjoy thinking about this analogy of the sea creature stripped
of its shell so it can grow. They may have felt that naked vulnerability when
it seems as if all the protective habits and patterns of a lifetime have been
stripped away.

One person, mentioned by Joyce Rupp in *Dear Heart, Come Home*,
described herself in the midst of the midlife transition as being like a huge
ocean liner "ponderously and laboriously trying to turn itself in a vast sea. It
can't turn quickly or with speed or make a sharp turn but turn it must. It
takes time to move this unyielding ship and when we finally do so we have
no idea where we are going!"[9]

Methodist minister James Harnish enjoys using the metaphor of traffic
and travel to describe the midlife journey. In his book *Men at Mid-Life:
Steering Through the Detours*, he writes that midway through their life
journey, men "are forced to stop in the traffic to check the road map, examine the directional signs, smell the fumes of their past, and determine where
in heaven's name they are going."[10] And why are men—and women, too—
forced to stop in the traffic of life and figure out where to go and what to do?

Harnish writes, "It's a story of detours that take us to places we never intended to go, unexpected people we bump into along the way, and dangerous potholes that threaten to damage the transmission." Then, later, after we have navigated the necessary changes, "we can take the wheel again with a better understanding of what makes this machine go, and a new excitement for what lies ahead."[11]

Harnish's use of the metaphor of detour is helpful, because most people find themselves feeling sidetracked by at least some of the events that happen between 35 and 55. The questioning and discomfort of midlife feels like an unwelcome interruption in a busy, forward-moving existence. Personal health issues, adolescent children, ailing parents, bifocals, and mammograms often feel like irritating and overly time-consuming intrusions into our productive lives.

Many metaphors are used to describe the drive to turn inward at midlife. This need for reflection and introspection has been likened to finding oneself in a cave, a well, a deep and tangled forest, a womb, a desert, or a tunnel. Some people compare the midlife transition to a butterfly emerging from its cocoon after living most of its life as a caterpillar.

Thinking about our life as a tree can also be helpful. In the first years of adulthood we focus on the visible part of the tree. Midlife involves turning from a preoccupation with the tree's branches and leaves to considering its roots. Are the roots well nourished? Are they well placed? What do the roots of my life need in order to provide nourishment to the tree so it can continue to grow branches and produce fruit during the second half of life?

Messengers of Midlife

Several writers talk about the "messengers" of midlife, those signs in our lives that inform us that something is going on and that it is now time to shed one of our shells, to stop and examine the roadmap, or to examine the roots of the tree that is our life. Two of the most common messengers of midlife are tears and sleeplessness. A normally optimistic and energetic person may find himself in tears more frequently. This occurs at unexpected times and is extremely disconcerting. A normally optimistic and energetic person finds herself tired and worn down because sleepless nights are becoming more common.

These are signs that some inner issues need attention. These are signs that the midlife transition is at hand and that it is now time to pay attention to past dreams, inner desires, and questions of meaning and purpose in life.

Other messengers of midlife include impotence, illness, depression, marital conflict, divorce, weight gain, job loss or dissatisfaction, and fatigue. All of these require attention.

I long for our congregations to be places where these difficult and uncomfortable signs can be validated and anticipated as harbingers of better things to come. These messengers of midlife are pointers that indicate approaching changes. And those changes can ultimately be very healthy and produce very good fruit.

Questions for Reflection

Questions for you to use personally in reflection, journaling, or discussion:

1. Many people experience a drive to turn inward at midlife, which requires increased time alone for thinking, journaling, praying, reflecting. Where are the spaces in your life when you can stop for reflection? What could you do to increase the opportunities for reflection?

2. What "messengers of midlife" are you experiencing? What messages are these messengers bringing to you? If your body could talk to you, what would it be saying? If you feel sadness or loss about something in your life, what is your grief telling you to do?

3. For women: Do you understand the biological changes involved in perimenopause and menopause? If not, consider buying and reading one of the many books available that explain what is happening in your body. Once you understand the biology of menopause, consider carefully what you are experiencing so you can discern which symptoms to discuss with your doctor and which ones to discuss with a spiritual director, pastor or rabbi, or therapist.

4. For men: Explore opportunities for growth in relationships. Consider joining a men's group. Consider taking up golf, an excellent sport for conversation. Explore ways you could be more intentional about relationships with your spouse, children, parents, siblings, relatives, neighbors, coworkers, and/or friends.

Questions for congregational leaders:

1. Spend some time alone or with other leaders evaluating the ways you currently minister to people between the ages of 35 and 55. List all the activities that people between 35 and 55 participate in. List all the possible ways these activities provide nurture, support, and growth opportunities for the people involved. You will probably find many aspects of congregational life that provide support and encouragement for this age group. Keep your list and use it as a baseline as you read this book, so you can consider areas for growth in the light of what you already do.

2. In what way do you make spaces in your worship and in your congregation life for reflection? Is there silence in worship? Are there classes or seminars on journaling or telling one's life story? Are there opportunities for contemplative prayer? Consider new ways you could affirm the turn inward that is so common at midlife.

3. In what ways do you as a congregation affirm the place of grief in human life? In what ways do you give permission for people to feel sad as they experience loss in their lives, or does your congregation imply that one's faith should always make them happy? Consider new ways you could come alongside people who are experiencing losses, which is so common at midlife.

CHAPTER 2

The Spiritual Issues of Midlife and How Congregations Can Help

My soul longs, indeed it faints, for the courts of the Lord;
my heart and my flesh sing for joy to the living God.

Psalm 84:2

On the weekday when I interviewed Burt in his home, the smell of baking bread filled the air. He had to interrupt the interview to pull the bread out of the oven. He told me he chairs the pastoral search committee at his church, and he always likes to bake fresh bread for their meetings.

"Taking time for this interview with you is evidence of the changes I've made at midlife," Burt said that day. He took me to his backyard, which was almost completely filled with a huge vegetable garden, to show me his workshop. A potter's wheel and kiln on one side of the room were splashed with clay, and a few unglazed pots stood on the worktable in the center of the workshop.

Burt showed me the path he has laid out, part cement walkway, part driveway, and part soft bark chips. The path completely circles his urban home, and features benches here and there. He likes to walk around his house, stopping to sit on the various benches and soak up the beauties of the physical world. His path reminds him of the cloisters in monasteries, where the monks walked laps while they prayed and meditated.

Burt, a physician, is 53. He spent most of his 40s as the assistant medical director for a consortium of hospitals. He worked 50 to 60 hours every week and traveled on many weekends. He went home each day with dozens of tasks left undone. He remembers, "I used all my energy all the time. I work very fast, but on any given day I couldn't get everything done. I could only get urgent things done. I was exhausted all the time."

At 50, Burt took a year's sabbatical from his job, with the goal of deciding whether to apply for the position of medical director, which he knew would soon become vacant. His high energy level is evident from the activities he undertook during his sabbatical. In that year, he trained to become a licensed massage therapist. He also created the workshop in his backyard by converting a shed into a comfortable space complete with a computer and woodworking tools, along with the pottery wheel and kiln.

In the middle of his sabbatical year, he put his hat in the ring for the position of medical director. Several months later, when he was one of the top six candidates, he withdrew his name. "I knew I could take on the position only if I felt called to do it," he says. "I came to realize the job would be very business-oriented, which would not be in harmony with my values. I thought a lot about my values during my sabbatical. And another one of my midlife issues was to stop taking responsibility for the whole and focus on something smaller.

"At midlife," he says, "you need to decide intentionally what needs to be done in the world and what part of it you can do."

Burt decided to go back into medical practice three-quarters time. In addition, he has taken on specific tasks at work: establishing a chronic pain service, overseeing the setup of the consortium's new computer system, and providing transitional support for the new medical director. He chose to take on these tasks because he was committed to them.

"I'm not as tired as I was," Burt reports. "I'm not as depressed as I was. Burnout and depression are caused by living a life that is not in harmony with your values. You don't do the things that build that vibrancy, that center of your self. I'm very busy, but I don't feel burnout is near. I find myself thinking, 'I've done 50; I'll have another 50.'"

Burt was raised Presbyterian, and he says in childhood he learned the importance of seeking the most meaningful spiritual experience, not just settling for what is most convenient. In his 40s he became more active in his Unitarian Universalist congregation, where now he and his wife regularly teach a popular six-week class called "Build Your Own Theology." It provides participants with the opportunity to explore their own beliefs and spiritual experiences in conversation with about a dozen others. Burt enjoys teaching the class because of his conviction that many people settle for the trappings of organized religion, rather than digging deeper to find meaning.

Each of the students in the class writes a "credo," a statement of what they believe. Every time Burt teaches the class, he writes a new credo, and he enjoys the opportunity several times each year to write down what is important to him.

Burt is convinced that our work and our finances have profound implications in our spiritual lives. If we want to explore the issues of values and meaning in our lives, it takes time, not just inclination. In our culture, Burt says, taking time for almost anything requires reducing work. We are caught in a cycle of working hard so we can consume more. We are unable to stop to consider what we are doing. Burt believes so many of us "are trapped and addicted to consumption. To find meaning in our lives, something has to mean more than just the gratification of immediate desire. The trap is that we believe we work very hard, therefore we deserve this purchase, this possession, this offsetting gratification."

He is committed to the idea of simplicity circles, where people get together in small committed groups to focus on simplicity and to discuss how to reduce addiction to things. Simplicity, he believes, is where the slack comes from in our lives so we can devote ourselves to the things that really matter to us. "Yet finding the slack isn't enough," he says. "You could use the slack time to sit around and read magazines." Developing that sense of mission, of purpose, is essential for emotional and spiritual health—figuring out "what needs to be done in the world and what part of it you can do."

Burt says, "People must get their family economics right in order to do what needs to be done in the world. My wife and I have our work pretty well aligned with what we value. We both work three-quarters time, and we could both make much more money elsewhere. In our culture, so many opportunities for spiritual richness within our communities and families are disallowed because of our drive for possessions. That's part of what you have to get straight at midlife."

The Spiritual Issues of Midlife

Almost every book on midlife discusses the fact that for many people, midlife is a time to grow and deepen spiritually. Burt's story illustrates some of the significant spiritual issues that often arise at midlife: the drive to discover our true values, the desire to figure out where and how we are called to serve in the world, the discovery of the joy of simplicity, and the need to create spaces of our own for "alone time," for silence, journaling, praying, or meditating.

There are many other spiritual issues that can arise at midlife. In the first chapter, we heard Will say, "In my early 40s, I was peeping over the hill looking at my own death." An increasing awareness that death is inevitable draws many people to consider questions of eternity and heaven. Others talk about letting go of the illusion of control. During the second half of life, many experience a new pattern of living characterized by open hands that are more receptive to what God is bringing into their lives. It is no longer possible to sustain the illusion that we are the ones ordering and controlling all the aspects of our lives.

Many midlife folks talk about a growing ability to live with ambiguity. Black-and-white thinking seems to fade away and people are more able to live with the tension of the complexities of life. This often includes developing a greater sense of mystery around issues of faith. People report dying to their previous understandings of God and growing in embracing the mystery and majesty of God.

Midlife is a time for facing old wounds and receiving healing. These wounds can include prior sexual abuse that we were not able to deal with in our teens or early adulthood, limits we placed on ourselves because of cultural or family values we received, or negative views of ourselves that we were unable to shake off in our 20s or 30s. A growing understanding of the redemptive nature of suffering often characterizes midlife. The joy that comes after working through some of these issues can give us great faith in the power of God to bring resurrection from death, to bring good things out of bad things.

Congregations Respond to Midlife

The issues described above often bring people back to the religion of their youth. Many congregations report growth in recent years, and at least part of that growth comes from new members who were not attending in early adulthood. Some are returning to their roots; others are seeking new paths.

In one Reform synagogue in the suburb of a large city, a significant number of men in their 30s and 40s are choosing to participate in a bar mitzvah. Often their interest is piqued when their sons are ready for their bar mitzvahs. Some of the men were raised in Jewish homes where there was no participation in a synagogue. Some of the men married Jewish women and want to learn more about the Jewish tradition. Either way, the turn towards spirituality so common at midlife is nurtured by this meaningful ceremony and the preparation that goes before it.

For people who have been attending a congregation more or less throughout adulthood, these powerful midlife forces often drive them towards deeper involvement. Many find increasing joy and contentment exploring spiritual issues in their community of faith. Some people who were infrequent attenders in their 20s and 30s find themselves more involved as they enter their 40s or 50s, and the increased involvement is meaningful and satisfying.

As congregations welcome new people in their 40s and 50s and encourage the deeper commitment of current members, it will be helpful to understand the significant spiritual issues of midlife so that programs can be tailored to meet those unique needs. First and foremost, congregations need to offer lots of entry points where people can meet others and talk about meaningful spiritual issues. Opportunities could include small groups focused on topics or on sharing, seminars on issues of everyday life, and seminars or classes on faith issues or the Bible. Effective entry points for people at midlife need to include significant opportunities for sharing, writing, or reflection. For example, an hour-long class on a book of the Bible could include 40 minutes of lecture and 20 minutes for small-group discussion. A class on the basics of faith could include an invitation for participants to write their own faith stories or their own statements of faith.

While we want to be aware of the need to welcome new people at midlife, it is also important to acknowledge that for many reasons, a good number of people become less involved in their congregations, or even leave, during their midlife years. Several rabbis told me they noticed a significant number of couples who became much less involved in the synagogue as their children left home. The challenge, they reported, was to develop congregational activities that engaged midlife adults for their own sakes, not just for the sake of their children.

A considerable number of people, many of them faithful members of congregations, feel abandoned and neglected in their midlife years. David Briggs, a writer for the Religion News Service, recently discussed the spiritual needs of midlife. He believes that churches, synagogues, and mosques have not been particularly effective at handling these needs.

As Briggs wrote, "Youth and the elderly have their own programs. Middle-aged folks are expected to be the bulwarks of religious institutions, teaching Sunday school and serving on church councils to keep the place running until they again take their place in the cycle of special ministries."[1]

He reported that some religious groups convey the idea that if you're a person of faith, you shouldn't have any kind of midlife crisis. This puts pressure on faithful congregation members to develop a mask of contentment to cover up the questioning and doubts inside.

Dropping the Masks

Phoebe would certainly agree that faithful congregation members feel pressure to appear happy even when they are experiencing the turmoil of midlife. Phoebe's midlife questioning was brought on by infertility. In her mid- to late-30s, Phoebe experienced the disappointment month after month of knowing she had not become pregnant.

"I got so angry at God," she remembers. "I found myself struggling constantly with the question of why there is pain in the world, and why God isn't more tangible in the midst of the pain."

Phoebe was accustomed to being a leader in her church. In those years of struggle, she wondered, "How could I tell people to pray when I couldn't pray? How could I communicate the importance of faith to people who are bitter and have barriers while I was struggling to get past my own barriers?"

Most of all, she felt so alone at church. It seemed that no one else was experiencing the kind of pain she felt, and no one welcomed the kind of questioning she was experiencing. She felt she had to hide what was going on and paste on a positive attitude.

Roxanne, a woman in her late 40s, reports experiencing the same feelings. Roxanne says that in the midst of intense midlife questioning, "the last place I could be honest was at church—not because of my current church but because of my childhood church. The best word to describe my church growing up is 'mask-y.' You always had to pretend everything was going well and that you were following the party line. I had a terrible time shaking off that attitude."

Both Phoebe and Roxanne report that a key turning point for them was when they began to be honest with God in their prayers, acknowledging their anger and pain. Roxanne says, "I decided I wasn't going to pray falsely. I began to believe that spirituality involved being honest with God and myself. I worked hard at that, and it was hard."

Phoebe says, "I began to feel free to yell in the midst of my anger and

I knew God heard me. In fact, when I yelled at God, I felt God smile. I felt like a little ant shaking my fist at God. But then I sensed God's pleasure and delight in all of me, including my anger."

Both Roxanne and Phoebe emphasize the importance of establishing an atmosphere in congregations where questions can be asked honestly. This includes support groups and other small groups in which people can share their experiences honestly and with vulnerability. People also need permission to be "real" in other settings, such as classes and committees.

Sermons that are real—with real problems and honesty on the part of the preacher—go a long way to helping promote an atmosphere that affirms the importance of questioning. Worship services that focus only on praise and do not include opportunities for confession and assurance of God's forgiveness are not helpful to people who are struggling. One of the arguments in favor of embracing the rhythm of the church year is that a variety of emotions are communicated through the ups and downs of the events we remember in different parts of the year. With careful thought, our worship services and our other activities can do more to communicate the importance of being honest before God.

The Turn Inward

Both Roxanne and Phoebe believe that slowing down and taking the time to turn inward helped them face God more honestly and move beyond the painful years. "Christianity for me always involved a lot of activity," Phoebe says. "Now a lot of the activity is gone and faith is imbedded in me more deeply. It is quieter and more honest."

Linda, in her late 40s, reflects, "In my 40s, as my kids needed me less and less, my career speeded up. I have more energy than I ever imagined. But I have found I need intentional time alone. I go to a monastery two or three times a year for a couple of days. I attend most of the services, and I spend a lot of time alone, reading and thinking. Those days have become an anchor for me. It is so refreshing to be alone for a time. I find I can't live without significant blocks of time to reflect."

"In the first half of my adult life, I was never alone in the house," says Ken, 53. "On my days off, my wife was always there, my kids were around. One of our kids is out of the nest and our younger son is usually working or out with friends. My wife is busier. Sometimes I have a whole day home alone. I can't believe how much I enjoy having the house to myself. I revel in it. The quiet envelops me and I feel such peace. Sometimes I study the Bible for a long period of time. Other times I read magazines or work in the garage. But there's something about being alone. . . . I never knew I would enjoy it so much."

"I get so angry when I go to church," says Kathleen, 45. "Everything the minister and the leaders say emphasizes the external aspects of faith: fellowship, sharing, praying in groups, service with a group of people. I've always been the quiet type, but I have been willing in the past to go along with this extraverted style of faith. Now I find I'm less tolerant. I believe my greatest gifts are praying for people and caring one-on-one for people. This small-scale, quiet kind of ministry is not affirmed at church at all. Why can't our congregational leaders acknowledge that personal faith and personal spiritual disciplines are just as significant as large-scale fellowship events?"

Idea for congregations:
Explore ways to affirm that personal prayer and meditation and quiet behind-the-scenes kinds of service are just as important as more visible, group-oriented manifestations of faith.

Many people report a turn inward at midlife. Sometimes it starts with the intense questioning about God that many experience. "Where is God?" we find ourselves asking. "Why don't I experience God more clearly?" These questions cause self-examination as we look inside ourselves for answers.

At midlife, many people also find themselves asking questions of meaning and purpose, which also contributes to a turn inward. "Who am I? What is my purpose in life? Why am I here? What should I do with the second half of my life?" We tend to look inward for answers.

Sometimes the turn inward simply manifests itself in an increased joy in being alone, in experiencing silence, in reflecting on life—past, present and future. For most people, the first half of adult life is characterized by a great deal of motion: establishing a career or a family or both, along with experimenting with our own competence by taking on a variety of activities. Sometime around age 40, many experience a drive to slow down and develop the inner life. The questions of midlife contribute to this drive inward, but even people who don't experience a lot of questions at midlife often experience increased joy in quiet activities.

This drive to turn inward can be extremely nurturing to faith. Prayer, meditation, and journaling can assume increased importance. People report that their faith grows deeper and feels more solidly a part of their inner being.

Congregations need to be intentional about affirming the significance of prayer, meditation, and journaling. I have observed a trend over my lifetime: Churches seem to have become more oriented to fellowship activities. When I was a child growing up Episcopalian, the service was characterized by lots of silence before and after. There was no passing of the peace. There were hardly any congregational activities such as picnics and dinners. This pattern was fairly consistent in the many Episcopal congregations we attended as we moved around.

Now, when I visit my parents' Episcopal congregation, I am always amazed at the number of activities that are planned. The same is true of my own Presbyterian congregation. These relational activities are wonderful, but they need to be balanced by equal opportunities to nurture the quiet activities of faith.

First and foremost, the congregational leaders need to be clear in their own minds that nurturing the quiet inner life of faith is significant and important. Do we affirm verbally in our services the significance of the ministry of prayer? Do we talk about the outer activities of faith—fellowship, witness, service—as being rooted in the inner and personal connection with God? Do we strive to develop a language about personal connection with God? Do we value prayer, meditation, and journaling as important spiritual activities? Do we use a period of silence in our worship services to model the necessity of an individual relationship with God? So many times, congregational leaders talk about all the activities that are coming up as if those activities constitute the only important aspects of the life of faith.

In addition, congregations can schedule activities that nurture the reflective life. Classes and seminars can help people learn to journal, pray, or meditate. Christian history is full of interesting material on contemplative prayer, which could be taught in a class or experienced in a contemplative prayer event. The Jewish tradition also offers many traditional practices that lend themselves to meditative prayer.[2] Overnight prayer vigils around Easter time offer an opportunity to pray alone in the church building and demonstrate the importance of prayer. Taking a group to a monastery can provide a rich model of the power of silence.

The Drive for Meaningful Service

At the beginning of this chapter we saw Burt's drive to find places to serve at church where he could express his conviction that many people settle for the trappings of organized religion, rather than digging deeper to find meaning. He enjoys teaching the class "Build Your Own Theology" because it provides participants the opportunity to explore and express what they have experienced in their spirituality and what they really believe. It provides a structure for them to dig deeper, and Burt is energized by participating in that process.

Burt first took the class in his mid-40s, and soon afterwards he and his wife began teaching it. It is not surprising that in his 40s Burt found a new avenue for service at church. Many others report discovering new paths of service at midlife.

I was 42 when I began to get involved with church finances. I had always enjoyed managing my husband's and my personal finances. When I was in my early 40s, my husband began his own business, and I found I greatly enjoyed managing the finances for him. When there was a gap at church in the area of financial management, I stepped in. I don't have a background in accounting, and I don't do well with small details around money, but I am very good at the big-picture aspects of finances: seeing patterns, communicating those patterns to the congregation, and overseeing the people who can track all the details.

What a surprise to find a new area of service in my 40s! I enjoy the feeling of mastery in a new area, but I also enjoy the way this aspect of service reflects my values. On a philosophical level, I am convinced that the way we use money reflects our deeply held values, and I want to do what I can to help congregation members understand the significance of their choices regarding money. On a much more practical level, I believe that we serve congregation members by keeping them informed about the congregation's finances. I enjoy this opportunity to act in accordance with values I didn't really know I had. I discovered the values that lay behind this service as I took on the new responsibilities.

My husband was 52 when he agreed to be a deacon in our Presbyterian congregation for the first time. Deacons provide caring ministries for people in need, both inside and outside the congregation. He loves this kind of service and wishes he hadn't waited so long to give it a try.

My mother was in her 40s when she began to volunteer at hospice, a totally new place to serve for her. She has grown immensely because of everything she has learned there.

Sarah was almost 40 when she realized her faith felt stale and all the avenues of service she had tried in her congregation seemed boring. In conversation with her pastor, she realized she had an embryonic interest in contemplative prayer. With his support and encouragement, she decided to pursue a certificate at the Shalem Institute in leading contemplative prayer groups.

After she received the certificate, the pastor encouraged Sarah to lead contemplative prayer groups at church. These groups have been a great asset to her congregation, and now two other people have stepped forward to help lead the groups. Sarah's story is a good illustration of the way a pastor or other congregational leader can help someone at midlife find a new and challenging place to serve.

Certainly some people find an area of service in their 20s and stick with that area for their whole lives. However, it is much more common for people to enjoy exploring new areas of service in their 40s and 50s. We need to encourage this kind of exploration in our congregations.

Most importantly, we need to make sure that people who have volunteered in one area for many years are given invitations to move to a new and different area of service. This relates to congregation members of all ages, but it is extremely important for people in the midlife years. Otherwise, these members may feel trapped in their current pattern of service. It takes a lot of self-direction or a lot of pain to stop doing something after long service. When some people finally muster up the courage to quit, their intense feelings of burnout may drive them away from the congregation because they believe there are no creative options there.

We can do a lot to avoid the pain of dramatic burnout by encouraging people to try new areas of service long before they burn out. We need to cultivate in our congregations an atmosphere of joyful experimentation in service. We need to talk more frequently about finding places for service that connect us with our values. In addition, we need to encourage people to develop mastery in areas that are new, long neglected, or long dreamed about.

Facing the Inevitability of Death

Many people report that they were in their 40s when they faced for the first time the reality that they would one day die. For some, this happens because of the death of a parent. For others, the beginning of the decline of their physical strength reveals to them a trajectory that leads downhill towards death.

Three Duke University professors have written a fascinating book entitled *The Search for Meaning*. In it, they explore the meaninglessness that is more and more prevalent in our society. They discuss the role of religion in our search for meaning. And they make the connection between the search for meaning and preparing for our own death. This connection seems to come to the surface at the time of midlife questioning.

They write, "Ultimately the search for meaning is concerned with planning the condition of our soul for the time of our death, when the spiritual, intellectual, emotional, and physiological dimensions of our life collapse into one." They believe we will find ourselves asking questions, such as "What will be our enduring legacy on earth? What is the essence of our lives? We must prepare ourselves for this final accounting through the never-ending search, always pushing our knowledge of life and death to the limit, always wrestling meaning out of meaninglessness."[3]

How can congregations help their members "prepare themselves for this final accounting?" As Will asks in chapter 1, "When's the last time you heard a sermon on preparing for death?" Congregation leaders need to wrestle with the idea that a significant number of people in our congregations are considering the meaning of their lives as they realize they will one day die. Then we can be more intentional about providing help with that wrestling.

A significant question that can be asked in conversations, small groups, and classes: What enduring legacy do you hope to leave? This certainly includes financial legacies, but it involves much more. How do you want to shape the world in the years remaining? What is most important to you? If you could do one thing for God, what would it be?

Another significant way to help people face the implications of their own death is to help them grieve the loss when family members or friends die. Congregations can offer seminars on the mourning process, with information on how to provide companionship for people who are grieving and for people who are dying. Seminars on grief and loss are especially appropriate during holiday seasons when loneliness is most acute.

Any kind of opportunity for reflection can provide opportunities to focus on issues of meaning. Many find it helpful to write an obituary for themselves. This could be done in the context of a class or seminar on any aspect of faith.

"Christmas is the worst time for me," says Lena, 44. "I feel like I'm too young to be an orphan, but my father died 15 years ago and my mother died when I was 40. She was my best friend. Every year the holidays come around and I am filled with loneliness for my parents. Last year during December, the church offered a Sunday morning class on coping with grief. There was a lot of sharing and I realized I wasn't alone. Lots of people have experienced the same kinds of losses I have. I began to understand that grief comes and goes. Just because I feel sad today doesn't mean I'll feel sad tomorrow."

Idea for congregations:
Offer a class or seminar on stages of grief, how to work through grief, and how to come alongside others who are grieving.

Letting Go of the Illusion of Control

"I like things organized," says Marie. "My life always went pretty much the way I planned it. I went to college, worked for a few years, got married, had kids. I stayed home with the kids and felt grateful to be able to do that. When Martin, my oldest, was in junior high, I went back to work half time, just the way I'd planned. It was hard when Martin was an adolescent, but I had expected some conflict, and it was pretty much the way I imagined it.

"But then Susan hit 14. She was completely out of control, smoking pot, getting into trouble at school, staying out too late at night. At the same time, the firm where my husband had been working relocated to Rhode Island, and he decided he didn't want to go. He was out of work for months. I bumped up my working hours to full time, but I was exhausted all the time. I never planned to work full time when I had kids at home. Then my mother got cancer, and she wanted me around all the time.

"After Rod went back to work, and I could cut back on my work hours and take some time to think, I realized I had always believed life could be controlled if I stayed organized enough. I learned it's all an illusion. People use that trite saying, 'Let go and let God.' I always thought it was stupid, but there's an element of truth in it.

"My mom's cancer is in remission. I'm so overwhelmingly grateful to have more years with her. She and I have gotten so much closer because of her illness. Susan is 19 now. She's still got a lot of growing up to do, but she's off drugs. She's become so sweet since she went away to college. During those really hard years with her, I had to give up my dreams about being close to my daughter. Now we are actually becoming friends. It is so precious and such a huge gift." With tears in her eyes, Marie added, "I feel like I live my life these days with open hands, grateful for the good things God gives me. Life is a gift, not a project to be managed. I never knew that before."

All sorts of unplanned events can shatter the illusion of control: issues around work, parenting, singleness, infertility, friendships, death, and the health of parents. Unplanned events seem to crowd more closely into our lives in our 40s than they did in our 20s. Perhaps the unfettered optimism of the 20s kept us from experiencing the events as deeply.

Congregational leaders can be on the lookout for people who are in the process of losing this illusion of control over life, in order to come alongside with careful listening and affirmation of the significance of what is happening. This transition from control to gratitude can be affirmed in congregational worship by using language such as, "We thank you, God, that in the unexpected events of life, you are constant."

This transition can be subtle but very significant. It is important to do all we can to encourage it when we see it.

Increased Comfort with Ambiguity and New Views of God

As people let go of the illusion of control, they usually find themselves becoming more comfortable with ambiguity in many areas. If life is primarily a gift, rather than a puzzle to be solved or a problem to be managed, then a lot of things that used to matter will cease to be as important.

People who used to be adamant about some aspect of life or faith may now become less certain they were right. As midlife folks become more certain of the core values they want to live by, the peripheral issues sometimes lose significance.

For some, this has a profound impact on their view of God. They find themselves asking new questions about God. The increased awareness of human suffering causes some to move away from a view of God as all-powerful or all-knowing. Maybe God relinquishes control of the universe, in some ways, into the hands of human beings, and thereby becomes less than omnipotent. Maybe God doesn't know everything in advance. Some may find themselves letting go of a view of God based on one image only—God as wrathful judge, Santa Claus, or miracle worker—to develop a picture of God that is more complex and nuanced.

God's tenderness and care for people in pain causes others, both men and women, to embrace female images of God. Some stick with the handful of female images of God in the Bible, and others go much further, addressing God with female names and using "she" and "her" with reference to God. Obviously, this can be very threatening to those of a more conservative persuasion. It is helpful to understand that these convictions sometimes come from the profound shifts taking place at midlife.

Facing Old Wounds

Ben was sexually abused by his church youth group leader when he was in his late teens. This came on top of a childhood filled with abuse in his family. Ben managed to lead a relatively healthy life until he reached his early 40s, although his painful past was manifested in the fact that he has stayed single because of his fears of intimacy.

Then he could go on no longer. Dating relationships just never worked out for Ben, and the residual pain from the abuse never went away. In fact, it seemed to grow in intensity. Finally, Ben told the story of his abuse to the pastor at his church. The pastor arranged for counseling for Ben at the church's expense. Because the abuse by the youth group leader had happened in that very same church, the pastor felt strongly that the church should pay for the counseling. It was arranged with complete confidentiality.

After a painful divorce and a cross-country move, David, 41, realized he wanted to find some kind of spiritual center for his life. He hadn't attended church since his childhood, but in his new location he began visiting neighborhood congregations. He settled at the Unitarian Universalist church in his neighborhood, largely because of a class called "Build Your Own Theology," offered regularly in that congregation. During the six-week class, members shared the stories of where they had encountered the sacred over the course of their lives. They each brought objects to the class— a rock, a feather, a religious symbol—that spoke to them of the sacred. And they each wrote a credo, a statement of what they believed.

Idea for congregations:
Offer places for people to tell their faith stories: small groups, seminars, classes. Offer places where people can wrestle with and articulate what they believe.

The fact that the church paid for the counseling was immensely healing for Ben. It was a sign that the church cared enough about him to try to undo what had happened to him earlier. The counseling itself was very helpful also. He was able to bring out into the open many issues and begin to move forward.

Ben's situation is not unique. Many of us stumble along through our 20s and 30s, coping well enough despite abuse or pain from childhood. In our 40s we may be called to deal with the pain. For some reason we simply can't keep it inside any longer.

There is a wonderful aspect about this drive to face old wounds and receive healing. For many, midlife is a time of discovering God as the tender healer who comes alongside us when we are in pain and the caring companion who accompanies us on the complex journey of life. We begin to understand experientially what the sages have always described as the redemptive character of suffering. We learn that God works good things in us when we face pain honestly and with hope.

Congregations can encourage this process by offering Twelve Step groups or sexual abuse recovery groups, led by trained people. Inner healing ministries, which use guided imagery to access and heal childhood pain, can also be very helpful. The congregational newsletter could publicize resources for recovery and healing and referrals to counselors, and the library could include books on healing and recovery. Sermons could include examples of people who have endured deeply painful situations.

As we look into the faces of people in our congregations, it is certain that at least some of them are facing issues from the past that are complex and weighty. We may not be able to see them, but they are there.

Human Creativity as a Reflection of the Creator

Many at midlife find increased joy in creative activities. Suddenly, more than ever before, they are able to experience God's presence as they draw, paint, quilt, play the piano, dance, garden, act in a play, sing in a choir, or write poetry.

I began writing fiction when I was 40, and it was like an "aha" experience for me. I felt connected to God as creator in incredible new ways. I was in awe of the whole creative process. My husband has taken up drawing and watercolor painting in his early 50s. He often signs up for classes at a nearby community college, and he has lots of fun getting books about painting and drawing out of the library. He has come to view God as the most accomplished artist, drawing and painting the creation day after day.

Connecting with God as creator through our own creative endeavors can be wonderfully healing to the soul. Memories of childhood pain often fall away in the face of a beautiful color or a particular evocative melody. When we are connected to something creative, we are often able to let go of our need to control, we experience awareness of a sense of eternity, and we are freed to express our inner world. Art, music, and writing often allow us to be honest with ourselves and with God in new ways. In fact, nurturing creativity can be an excellent way to experience many of the midlife spiritual growth patterns described in this chapter.

It may be threatening for clergy and congregational leaders to realize that some of their members encounter God more fully when writing poetry or painting than they do in formal worship. Yet we can affirm the presence of God in creative activities as we also affirm the significance of congregational worship and service.

The Growing Edge for Congregations

The midlife journey takes similar form in people's lives, whether they are conservative or liberal Christians, Jews, or Unitarians. Some of the same kinds of questions and issues arise. Some of the same difficult feelings appear: meaninglessness, fear in the face of death, discouragement at the loss of physical strength, questions about God and faith. Some of the same healthy desires also appear: the drive to spend more time alone, the longing to discover deeply held values and to act in accordance with those values. While the path of midlife is similar in various faith traditions, different parts of the midlife search have unique implications in different communities of faith.

In conservative Christian circles, the questioning can be particularly threatening. The growing ability to live with ambiguity and the distrust of black-and-white answers can be difficult for congregation members and leaders to accept. Some congregation members and leaders in conservative churches will probably be uncomfortable with people at midlife who desire to embrace feminine aspects of God's character. In conservative Christian churches, more than in any other setting, it is sometimes communicated that the questioning of midlife is inappropriate, because if a person truly has faith, then he or she wouldn't experience this turmoil.

In some liberal Christian churches and in Unitarian Universalist churches, people at midlife may need a degree of certainty in matters of faith that will make others uncomfortable. Midlife is a time of searching and questioning, but when people come through to the other side of midlife, they will probably have some truths they are adamant about. This may feel uncomfortable in some congregations.

One Unitarian Universalist pastor near retirement described the pattern he had observed over and over in different congregations. New people come to the congregation. They are in their 20s, fed up with the rigidity of the church in which they were raised. They love the openness in the Unitarian congregation. They spend their 20s and early 30s reacting to their memories of the church of their childhood. By the time they reach their late 30s, they are ready to figure out what they really believe for themselves, quite apart from everything they have been rejecting for a decade or more. And they are sometimes surprised at the strength of their convictions about what they do believe. And their fellow members might also be surprised!

In the Jewish tradition, age is viewed positively. Elders have always been valued for their wisdom. Some Jews may find that people at their temple are impatient with midlife questioning. It is viewed as an unfortunate manifestation of the Christian culture rather than a legitimate life transition that can have positive results.

How Congregations Can Help

Congregational leaders, first and foremost, can come to understand the variety of significant spiritual issues so real to many in the midlife years, issues that will have implications on programming, recruiting for service, and countless other small areas.

We have special programs for children, youth, and young adults. We also have special programs for seniors. The people in between are often viewed as the workhorses of the congregation. Yet the period of life from 35 to 55 is an extremely rich time of exploration, growth, and discovery. It is not some sort of flat holding pattern that we call adulthood but should ignore in our congregational ministries.

When we interact with people in that age group, we can expect to discover that they are learning interesting things and growing in faith. They are facing challenging life events that come from outside themselves, such as parenting adolescents, coping with the aging or death of parents, and dealing with a whole raft of issues such as infertility, job loss, and the empty nest. They may also be finding new and challenging desires coming from inside them, such as longing for a sense of purpose in the face of the reality of death, a desire for solitude, and a multitude of questions about personal values and the meaning of life.

These challenges, whether driven by outer events or inner forces, provide excellent opportunities to help people discover meaning and values through their faith and their religious tradition. We can help people at midlife grow through these rich years by:

- addressing issues around mourning and grief
- helping people think about their legacy and prepare for their own deaths

- providing opportunities for honest sharing on a variety of topics
- being "real" in sermons and classes
- affirming the inner journey as well as outer service and activities
- providing opportunities for journaling/writing in classes and seminars
- providing opportunities for people to explore a variety of ways to serve
- giving long-time volunteers the opportunity to move to other, new areas of service
- affirming the need for healing of past wounds
- encouraging development of new views of God
- affirming the place of creative activities in the life of faith

---

"I was sexually abused by a cousin when I was 10," says Nina. "I was 40 before I told my parents about it. I needed lots of support in those difficult months when I was deciding whether or not to talk about it, and I found that support in my congregation. There was a group of women who included me. We met weekly for over a year. Several of us had significant issues around sexual abuse, and we supported each other through a lot of struggle and healing as we dealt with it. I'll always be glad those women were there for me."

Idea for congregations:
Form a support group for people dealing with past sexual abuse.

Congregations may also want to offer a class or seminar on the subject of midlife. Several of the people I interviewed indicated that it would have helped them a lot if their congregation had offered an arena to explore midlife issues so they wouldn't have felt so alone when questions arose in their own minds. They also said that they were surprised by the issues that arose in their lives. If they had known ahead of time that those issues would probably arise, it would have helped them a lot, they believed.

As we will see in the next chapter, family issues often provide opportunity for congregations to invite people to explore midlife spiritual issues. Talking with parents of adolescents about parenting issues provides an excellent opportunity to describe some of the midlife issues that often arise when our children reach adolescence. We will see that marriage enrichment events also provide an opportunity for midlife issues to be mentioned. Groups or events for singles in their 30s also provide a setting where midlife could be discussed. These settings could be used very effectively and naturally to present and discuss midlife issues.

The growing edge for congregations is to take seriously the reality of their members' midlife journeys. Many between 35 and 55 will be dealing with loss in whole new ways. Many will be exploring questions of meaning and purpose. Many will find themselves drawing near to God in new ways. Many will be feeling a need for freshness, for experimentation, for new spiritual patterns and new ways to serve. This is a great opportunity.

Questions for Reflection

Questions for you to use personally in reflection, journaling, or discussion:

1. Which of these spiritual issues, typical at midlife, have been a part of your life? In what ways have they drawn you closer to God? In what ways have they pushed you further away from your faith/spirituality?

    • the drive to discover deeply held values
    • the call to meaningful service
    • the joy of simplicity
    • the need for time alone
    • facing the reality of death
    • letting go of the illusion of control
    • growing ability to live with ambiguity
    • greater sense of mystery and awe
    • new views of God
    • facing old wounds and receiving healing
    • human creativity as a reflection of the Creator

2. Pick one of the above issues and live with it for a period of time, maybe a week or a month. Keep your eyes open for newspaper and magazine articles, TV shows and movies, novels and nonfiction that relate to the issue. Talk with your friends about it. Pray and meditate about it.

3. Write a personal philosophy that addresses the values you believe are important. Write a personal statement of faith or credo that expresses what you believe about God and life.

Questions for congregational leaders:

1. Look at the list of issues under question 1 above. Consider what your congregation does or doesn't do to help people grapple with each of the issues. Pick one or two of the issues that you are particularly concerned about and brainstorm ways your congregation could address those issues more intentionally.

2. Consider where in your congregation you could provide opportunities for people to write a personal faith history, a personal philosophy, or a personal statement of faith. Consider where in your congregation people could tell their faith story.

3. Reread the section above, "How Congregations Can Help." Evaluate your church programming in the light of the list in that section.

CHAPTER 3

Family Matters

The Lord upholds all who are falling, and raises up all who are bowed down.

Psalm 145:14

"A lot of what we call midlife is related to the stress of having teenagers," says Marcie, the mother of two teenage boys. She has watched the other parents of teenagers in her church band together in small support groups as their children entered this complex age and stage. "In fact, the timing of midlife depends on whether you had children early or late. If you had kids when you were young, then you will be younger when they enter adolescence and you will experience midlife earlier, too."

"Midlife is about stripping away," says Rita. "For single people like me—who have never been married and who don't have children—this stripping away is very different than for married people. Married people have to face the fact that their dreams haven't turned out like they expected. For single people, it's harder. We have to acknowledge that we will probably never have what we've dreamed of. And we find ourselves asking why God wouldn't want to give us our dreams. How can we possibly believe God hears our prayers?"

"Congregations need to realize that people are going through real issues," Donna reflects. Donna got married at 27 and began trying to get pregnant at 31. At 39, she and her husband were able to adopt a child. The years of her mid-30s, when she was battling infertility, were dark and lonely. "Midlife raises lots of questions," she says, "and that's normal. Our culture tempts people to cover up the pain with relationships, drugs, and so on. Congregations need to be places where people can acknowledge midlife and ask questions and not receive black and white answers. Gray has become a very important color in recent years for me."

"I've lost my lighthouse, my north star," says Ken, 53. "My father was the one person who loved me unconditionally all my life. He supported me when I made some really stupid choices. He prayed for me every day of his life. And now he's gone. He died more than two years ago, but I still miss him all the time. I feel like a child again, cast adrift in a rowboat with no lighthouse to guide me."

These four people are describing some of the significant family issues at midlife. For Marcie, midlife centers around parenting two boys who are separating from her very rapidly. She is losing her job, her role. For Rita, midlife centers around the loss of lifelong dreams of marriage and motherhood, and she feels distant from God. For Donna, her midlife passage consisted of depression regarding the issue of infertility. Ken has the sense of starting life over without his dad, straining to find other lights to guide him.

While these are some of the common family issues that impact our congregation members at midlife and trigger questions about faith, there are countless other family patterns. One 46-year-old woman laughs about beginning menopause while she is parenting a toddler and a preschooler and is in the midst of nurturing her career and trying to keep up with friends who have teenagers. Her life feels squeezed and jam-packed. Every minute is spoken for, and she lives each day trying to faithfully meet the needs of her children, her husband, and her clients, with the occasional moment for her own needs. Yet she knows she is doing everything she wants to be doing. One father in his early 50s with a very young family seldom takes the time to think about career questions—or any questions at all—because he also is too busy with the needs of the children and his job.

The prevalence of divorce and remarriage has also changed the face of midlife. Two 40-year-olds, friends from high school, get back together and decide to get married. The husband has joint custody of his two children from a previous marriage. The wife has never been married and becomes a stepmother and a wife simultaneously, right at the same time that she is starting a new career.

At 43, Wendy has just divorced her husband. She has custody of their two children and is learning to be a single person again after 16 years of marriage. She observes huge differences between single people her age who have never been married and those who were once married, particularly if they have children. She says their view of sexuality, of what they desire in a relationship, and how they view dating are completely different.

The Losses Pile Up

One therapist says that a defining characteristic of the midlife years is that
the losses pile up, and we become more competent in facing loss and learning to live with the reality that another loss could be just around the corner.
We grow in our ability to take joy in the present, with gratitude for this
moment, because we know that nothing lasts forever. Because the losses
pile up and because we have endured them and tried to cope with them, we
are changed people.

What I'm calling the "family issues" of midlife center around loss: loss
of dreams, loss of relationships, and loss of roles. Some of these losses
seem obvious: the single woman at menopause who realizes she will never
bear a child, the man in his 50s grieving the loss of his father, and the empty
nest couple who are enjoying being a couple again but also feel the loss of
their children's presence. Some of the losses are more subtle, such as the
loss of companionship felt by a father when his fourteen-year-old son no
longer wants to go to baseball card conventions with him.

Many of the losses people experience during the midlife years have
nothing to do with family. I was 41 when I lost my closest friend from my
young adult years to cancer. At a recent midlife seminar I asked if anyone
had lost a friend to death, and almost everyone raised a hand. I asked them
if they had experienced the death of a friend when they were in their 20s,
and only a few responded.

The loss of career dreams and physical strength, both common at midlife,
also have little to do with family. However, these losses accumulate. When
we add these losses to the ones experienced around family issues, the losses
do indeed "pile up" for most people during the midlife years. We need to be
aware of the reality of loss as we try to serve the people in our congregations.

In this chapter we will look at four major midlife family issues: singleness, parenting adolescents, nurturing marriage, and coping with aging and
dying parents. We will consider the midlife questions raised by each of
these situations, and we will explore ways congregations can help their
members face the losses involved. Even though we focus on these four
areas, we will also try to be aware there are many midlife folks in family
situations that don't fit neatly into these categories.

Susan, 41, is single. Both of her parents died when she was in her 30s. Her sister and brother live in other parts of the country. Susan is a confident bank manager with an active life, but the holidays are very difficult for her. She says, "If only congregations could offer a way for people to get together on holidays. Oh, I don't mean a way to sign up to go to someone's home. That feels just as awkward, as if I'm intruding. I'd like a gathering at a restaurant, where we can eat together and talk for a while, and then go home. I'd also like the opportunity to host people at my apartment. Otherwise I never take the time to decorate for the holidays."

Idea for congregations:
Consider the needs of single people at the holidays. Provide opportunities for single people to gather at a restaurant or to host others in their home.

Singleness at Midlife

"The church has dealt poorly with singles," says Rita, 42. "So much of the focus is on families, with Sunday school classes, parenting classes, family fun events. Those of us who are single have to struggle to find a place. People talk about the church becoming a family, but this is a huge challenge for those of us who feel different and a little bit inferior because we have never been married."

Rita has been employed by the same insurance company for almost 20 years. She is competent and articulate in a quiet way, and she has worked her way up to a significant management position. She is also a committed athlete and competes in mini-triathlons every year. However, relationships are the cutting edge of her life and the area she spends the most time thinking about.

"You become friends with someone," she reflects. "You spend time with them and you want the best for them, so of course you want them to meet someone and get married. But when it happens, it's hard to maintain the friendship. When my friends marry, most of them have children right away, and that creates a huge change in my relationship with them. There's a constant sense of loss.

"I've heard married people say that midlife issues are the same for single and married people, that it's all about unfulfilled dreams. I think single people experience a kind of stripping away that is very different than married people face. You married people got to experience your dreams. You may not like them, but you got them. We single people didn't get to have our dreams."

For Rita, midlife is complicated by the fact that early menopause runs in her family. At 42 she has completed menopause. She says, "My sister told me menopause was no big deal, but I told her that she already has a family so of course it's no big deal for her. For me, menopause has forced me to give up the dream of having my own children. Also, it's really hard to be involved in dating relationships and to realize that one thing you can't offer this man is the possibility of having children with him. It makes me feel that I have much less to offer someone, and that hurts."

Rita says she watches her single friends in their 40s struggle with feeling crushed. They wonder if God has heard their prayers. They wonder if somehow they have missed God's will. Or can singleness be God's will?

"I find myself thinking, 'God's will should feel better than this,'" Rita says. "It seems to me the task of midlife is to adjust to the fact that life isn't what we expected it to be and God's will isn't either. I've been learning to focus on God walking us through these struggles rather than God bailing us out. We need to cling to the truth that God is good.

"I find myself investing more in people and less in agendas," Rita reflects. "Life is messy. I'm more committed to helping people in the midst of mess, rather than always trying to fulfill my agenda. The more I deal with the mess of life, the more I recognize what Jesus was doing in talking with lepers and prostitutes. I'm trying to see people as they are—and most people are in pain—and I find God there."

Rita's ability to focus on God waxes and wanes in the midst of her pain as a single person who will never have biological children. In her good moments, she is able to be thankful for the benefits of her freedom as a single person. At other times, she is in tears because of her sense of loss.

It's easy for a married woman juggling the demands of husband, children, home, and job to be envious of Rita's trim, athletic build and her quiet competence. As congregational events are planned, it's easy to forget the special needs of single people. Rita's story reminds us that even people who appear competent and successful on the outside may be struggling to maintain faith that God is good and that God is working in their lives. And those of us who are married need to remember that even the most content single person struggles with the loss of friendships when friends get married.

Of course, not all single people feel the same grief and loss that Rita feels. We cannot assume that just because someone is single, he or she always wanted to be married and feels crushed to still be single. However, I have frequently heard concerns similar to Rita's. What she has experienced is not unusual.

The midlife issues for single people who were once married are significantly different from those for single people who have never married. Consider Ron, also 42, who was divorced at age 39 after 10 years of marriage. In the last years of his marriage, he watched his wife fall in love with someone else. All the intimacy they had experienced slowly dissipated, and he watched her light up in the presence of the other person.

For Ron, singleness at 40 precipitated a crisis in confidence. He wonders if he has what it takes to maintain a relationship over the long haul. He sees that he neglected some of the tender romantic gestures that might have enabled his wife to continue to love him. He wonders if he will do any better the second time around. He finds it hard to talk to people in his congregation about his fears in the relational realm.

In contrast, Wendy experiences being single as a huge relief. After 14 years in a difficult marriage, she feels great peace now that she's been divorced for a year. She is energized and enthusiastic about her life. She also finds it hard to talk with people in her congregation about how she feels. She doesn't want to criticize her husband to people who have known him in the congregation, but the truth is that there were many abusive aspects to their marriage. She knows that her contentment and joy are threatening to people in her congregation who believe that marriage should last a lifetime.

Wendy's story illustrates that we cannot make assumptions about people. A recent divorce does not guarantee that someone will be miserable. Wendy definitely still needs the support and affection of congregation members, but her experience of loss occurred inside her marriage rather than after the marriage ended.

The holidays are particularly challenging for single people. One woman makes it her goal to pray regularly for single people during the holidays. Congregations can make a point of helping people get together for holiday meals.

Careful use of language in congregational publications can also help single people. Take some time to read over your church newsletter and

Rita, 42, has already gone through menopause, which is normal for the women in her family. As a single woman, menopause was a huge event for her because it meant the end of her dream of having a baby. She finds herself feeling brittle and hypersensitive every time the word "family" is mentioned. She says, "I came to church one Sunday morning in the summer. It turned out the first service was scheduled to be held in the fellowship hall with breakfast served. The sign on the church door read, "Family Service in the Fellowship Hall." I saw the word "family," and I felt despairing that I would ever have a family, and I started to cry. So I just left and went home. I know it's stupid, but that's how I felt."

Idea for congregations:
Carefully examine the language you use to promote events. Because of the rise in infertility and because of the large number of single people, be careful how you use the word "family." It is a word that can make couples without children and single people feel unwelcome.

brochures with the eyes of a single person. Does the word "family" occur too often? Are there activities to which single people are clearly welcomed?

In addition, go beyond the issue of language to look at the substance of your church programs. Look for opportunities to offer intergenerational events rather than family events, and advertise them that way. In my own church the children's ministries department recently rented an ice skating rink on a Sunday afternoon. Because I knew who was organizing the event, I foolishly assumed only families with children would be attending. Everyone else read the promotional fliers accurately and knew that it would truly be an intergenerational event. Seventy people of all ages attended, making it one of our more successful social events. I was sorry I hadn't wobbled around on the ice with everyone else!

Parenting Adolescents

Bob and his teenaged son David argue a lot. David enjoys playing the guitar, and Bob feels that David puts too much time into music and not enough time into homework. David gets good grades, but not straight As.

Laura, David's mother and Bob's wife, is proud of David's grades and observes that he always gets his homework done even if he has to stay up late to do it. Bob wants David to change this pattern of late-night homework. Bob wants David to do his homework first and have fun second. Bob believes David is capable of perfect grades and feels angry that David won't work for them.

Bob says, "It's not that I mind the guitar playing. It's just that he needs to have a sense of priorities. Work comes first, fun comes second. I wish it was different and that I didn't have to carry home a briefcase full of paperwork every night." Bob wishes he could relax and fool around with his stereo at night, but he can't because he needs to tackle all that paperwork he brings home.

"I'm just trying to show him what real life is like," says Bob. "He's going to have to learn sooner or later. He might as well learn it now."

Psychologist Laurence Steinberg recounts this story about Bob, Laura, and David in his book *Crossing Paths: How Your Child's Adolescence Triggers Your Own Crisis.*[1] Steinberg's book presents his research about the effects on parents of their children's adolescence. He says that most studies focus on teenagers who are not doing well. Steinberg wanted to focus on parents. He was curious about the effects on the parents when their children enter into the complex growth stage of adolescence.

In his interviews with Bob, Steinberg came to understand what Bob was feeling. "*He* wasn't having very much fun. His work was time-consuming but not especially satisfying, and he resented his 'homework'—his 'briefcase full of paperwork.'" Bob was feeling financially stretched and taken for granted by David, "so he had begun to transfer his dissatisfaction about his life—his dissatisfaction about not having enough 'fun'—into resentment about David's leisure time. It was not at all surprising that David's homework had become the focus of Bob's irritation."[2]

This pattern of transferring our own dissatisfaction with our lives into conflict with our teenage children is one of many patterns cited by Steinberg. He talks about the man with a routine job who loved collecting baseball cards with his son. They attended baseball card conventions together and spent hours arranging their collection. When the son entered adolescence and lost interest in baseball cards, the father felt bereft. He had lost a friend, a relationship.[3]

Diana, 43, is attending a class required by her church for parents with children making the transition from elementary school to junior high. She attended the class four years earlier, when her daughter was approaching adolescence. Most of what she heard that time seemed irrelevant because she was unwilling to believe her daughter would ever become rebellious. Now she knows differently, and she is listening intently, wondering what is ahead for her 12-year-old son. At the end of the class, she reflects, "Now I understand that my kids and I are going through the same thing. We are trying to decide who we are. We're trying to separate from our parents' values and priorities, so we can establish our own. That gives me much more sympathy for my kids. And it makes me want to be gentle with myself in this time of midlife questioning."

Idea for congregations:
Offer classes for parents of adolescents. Help the parents understand the parallels between the issues of adolescence and the issues of midlife.

Steinberg talks about the mother whose life revolved around the needs of her children. As her daughter, her youngest child, became more independent in adolescence, the mother was shut out of her life. The mother lost a relationship she had cherished. In addition, she lost a role. She was no longer needed to help with clothes shopping, to drive her daughter around, to lovingly prepare lots of meals for her daughter. She felt bereft and disoriented.[4]

Steinberg notes it is not unusual for parents to feel jealous of their adolescent children. In the story of Bob and David, some of Bob's irritation with David's study habits came from sheer jealousy that David had so much discretionary time. As adolescent children enter into the world of dating, it is not unusual for parents to feel some amount of jealousy—particularly towards a child of the same sex—as the teen begins to meet and spend time with attractive members of the opposite sex.[5]

Jealousy of physical prowess is also not uncommon.[6] Teenagers are growing into their adult strength at the same time that their parents are beginning to decline in strength. Parents who have always enjoyed athletic activities with their children may feel shut out when children grow beyond the parents' strength and athletic competence level. Parents may feel jealous that their child can look ahead to years of increasing strength, while the parent can only look ahead to continuous physical decline.

The empty nest marks a huge landmark for parents. What many parents do not realize is that the empty nest is a process that begins quite a few years before the children leave home. Steinberg reports that most parents, particularly mothers, experience more psychological turmoil during the years before their children leave home than after they leave.[7] In fact, for many women, while they do miss their children, the empty nest represents an opportunity to pursue individual interests.

The parents' psychological turmoil before the empty nest usually starts somewhere around the beginning of their child's adolescence, when most children enter into a period of disrespect for their parents. Suddenly their parents are no longer very smart, knowledgeable, or cool. For those parents who have enjoyed having an almost godlike stature in their children's lives, this step is painful indeed.

Then come the years of growing independence. The teenagers want to stay out later. They want to choose their own clothes. They don't want to hear advice on any subject. If they get a driver's license and have access to a car, they may almost disappear from family life.

These changes often cause tremendous anxiety for parents. It is frightening to watch someone who was a baby in your arms only a few years ago drive away in a car for the first time. Even if a teenager is faithful about obeying curfew rules, it is frightening not to know exactly what he or she is doing as the hours grow later on a Friday night. These anxious feelings are a normal part of parenting as children make the transition from childhood to adulthood.

Steinberg's research is so helpful because he helps us see that many of the emotions we feel in the face of adolescent children are rooted in the realities of our own lives. In many cases, the parents of teenagers are losing a significant role or an important relationship that has filled many hours of their lives. In many cases, the parents are experiencing loss in their own lives—loss of physical strength, loss of unfulfilled dreams, loss of their view of themselves as powerful, sexually attractive people—and those losses are compounded by what they see in the lives of their children.

As congregational leaders make conscious choices to minister to parents of adolescents, they would do well to consider what Steinberg said as he reflected on the surprising level of openness and responsiveness that he experienced with parents during his research. At first he thought that parents were so willing to participate in his study because they desired information about how to better understand their teenagers. He writes, "What I did not realize was that many parents participated in our project not because they did not understand their child, but because they were confused about what was happening to themselves."[8]

Any event for parents of teenagers—whether it's a class, seminar, or any kind of support group—should include some opportunity for reflection about the ways the presence of teenagers in the family impacts the parents. For example, in my own congregation a very successful seminar addressed the topic of how to talk to your teenager about sex. A therapist discussed issues such as conveying information about sex to children and teens, appropriate boundary setting for teens, and how to keep the communication lines open. In addition, she allowed time for discussion about the ways that the emergence of teenage sexuality raises issues in the parents. This second piece is essential.

Unresolved issues from our own adolescent years may arise as we watch our children become sexually aware. Our own doubts about our sexual prowess may come to the surface as we see our teenagers begin to date. Our fears about sexual decline as we get older may become more visible as we see the vibrant beauty of teenagers. The therapist who presented the seminar at our church did an excellent job of communicating that these feelings may very well arise right at the same time that we are struggling to set appropriate boundaries for our teenagers. She conveyed to the parents a sense of permission and openness in facing these complex issues. She helped the parents know that they are not alone in these confusing feelings.

Watching teenagers discover their sexuality can bring many memories and feelings to the surface as parents remember their own teenage years. And sexuality is not the only area triggered by watching adolescents. For many people, adolescence was a period of difficult and significant decisions. In the busy years of the 20s and 30s, many parents did not take the time to think back on those decisions and the ways they impacted so many aspects of life.

Parents sometimes experience the emergence of many powerful memories and emotions as they watch their teenage children learn to navigate life on their own. They may feel profound and intense regret about some of the choices they themselves made, choices which have repercussions every day. Anyone who leads a class, seminar, or group experience in a congregation—on any subject—needs to be aware of this process of life review that is probably going on in the lives of parents of teenagers. Opportunities for discussion, journaling, meditation, and/or reflection need to be incorporated into every learning experience so people can process what is happening in their own lives and apply the truths of their faith to their own situation.

Marcie, who was mentioned at the beginning of this chapter, sees close connections between midlife issues and parenting teenagers. The life review process that is prompted by watching teenagers grow up raises many

Marion, 45, recently attended a Saturday morning seminar at her church entitled, "How to Talk with Teens about Sex." The course was taught by a therapist who has three children in their twenties. With her children's permission, the therapist illustrated the seminar with lots of stories from her own parenting experience. Margy's own midlife journey has included growing awareness of the odd sexual climate in her family of origin. There was no sexual touching, but inappropriate nakedness and sexual banter was very upsetting to her. She managed to submerge her uncomfortable memories in the busy years of parenting small children, but at midlife, as her children entered adolescence, the painful memories demanded attention. The principles of appropriate sexual boundaries in parenting, presented by the therapist, and the discussion with other parents were very healing for Margy.

Idea for congregations:
Offer a class, a seminar, or open discussion on talking with teens about sexuality.

of the midlife issues we have already discussed: I see my children making a lot of decisions, and I find myself wondering, did I make good decisions when I was their age? Have I used the first half of my life wisely? What am I going to do with the second half? What do I really value? Now that my kids don't need me very much, where am I going to put my energy? Where do I really want to serve? How can I receive healing for the hurts I experienced in my own adolescence?

Certainly the illusion of control is shattered when we enter into the realm of parenting teenagers. And many parents of teenagers will tell you that their prayer life has become more intense, particularly on Friday and Saturday nights, when they fervently pray that their teenagers will be protected from harm. Parents of teenagers have to relinquish their children into the hands of God because they can no longer be there every minute to protect their children. This pattern of relinquishment may help parents experience the truth that there is actually no area of life over which they have complete control. It becomes more clear that it is a good idea to relinquish everything we are and have into God's hands.

In Marcie's church many parents of teenagers have come together to form small groups. In fact, that church's small-group ministry has been revitalized by this drive for support on the part of parents of teenagers. Small groups are an excellent forum to discuss issues that emerge as children enter adolescence because they provide opportunities for discussion, reflection, and support. Parents can pray together in small groups for their children and for their own issues that have been raised by having teenagers in the family.

I know I experienced shame as the parent of teenagers when my kids didn't seem to be conforming to some external standard of success. Shame breeds in isolation. That's one reason why it is so important to get parents of teenagers together, whether in small groups, classes, or seminars. Every opportunity for gathering together should include some component that addresses parenting skills, along with time for discussion or reflection on the personal issues raised by parenting teenagers.

Marriage: The U-Shaped Curve of Marital Satisfaction

Numerous studies have shown that marital satisfaction—on the average—goes down with the birth of the first child, continues to go down with the birth of each succeeding child, and then goes back up at the time of the empty nest. Congregational leaders would do well to spend some time thinking about the implications of this pattern.

"My husband and I have been having a great time in the past two years," says Linda, 46, whose teenage sons are 17 and 19. "It was just about two years ago that our older son got very busy with work and friends.

At the same time, our younger son got an internship on Saturday evenings from six to midnight. We could go out every Saturday night! We rediscovered dinners out. We often went for a walk right at sunset. Sometimes we went to a movie. It was wonderful to be able to plan ahead for Saturday night social events.

"The years before he got that internship were difficult. Both boys would always make their weekend plans at the last minute. Saturday night might involve five boys spending the night at our house—all of it arranged at dinner time on Saturday. As much as possible, we tried to be at home on weekend nights. It felt a little bit like prison.

"After about eight months at the internship, our younger son quit because it was interfering with his social life too much. From that time on, he has been out with his friends on Saturday nights. So my husband and I have continued to enjoy lots of time together. Even though our nest isn't empty yet, we are having that renaissance of our marriage that you so often hear about. It's been wonderful."

Sarah and Kevin have children at about the same age as Linda's children, but their story is quite different. Kevin says, "Somehow we drifted apart during the years that we had small children. I was working hard building my business. Sarah wanted to be home with the kids, but she really missed working. Being at home did something to her self-image and she became a little depressed. I got more distant and busy with work, while she became sadder and more convinced that I really didn't love her. A few years ago we began marriage counseling, which brought a lot of the issues out into the open.

"We're working on the issues, trying to talk more often and more openly. Now that the kids are older, we can leave them at home and go out for a cup of coffee or for a meal. That has helped us feel closer, but we still remember years of painful interactions. That still makes it hard to be really honest with each other."

Even though, on the average, couples experience greater marital satisfaction at the time of the empty nest, some couples struggle at that time because they no longer have their children as a focus of their marriage. Sarah and Kevin are optimistic that they will have increased their ability to communicate by the time the kids leave, so that they can enjoy being together—just the two of them. In order to experience that peace and acceptance in each other's presence, they have a lot of work to do.

Another issue that couples face during midlife, particularly if they have been married 10 or 20 years, is the need to negotiate the significant changes that either or both individuals have experienced. "She's not the woman I married," the husband finds himself thinking, and he is right. The woman who happily stayed home with kids is now the vice president of a mail-order business. The husband who happily worked long hours to be a good provider now wants to slow down, smell the roses, develop his golf game, and spend time fishing with his brother.

Congregations need to do whatever they can to encourage healthy marriages. Marriage enrichment events can offer a format that encourages couple interaction to discuss the issues mentioned in this chapter. In addition, these kinds of events can help congregation members to remember that a healthy marriage requires nurture and attention.

Another congregational program that encourages marital growth is a marriage mentoring program. Couples who have been married more than 10 years are matched with engaged or newly married couples. The benefit goes both ways. The younger couples benefit from the discussion with the couple who has been married longer. But the mentor couple also benefits.

Many couples who have served as mentors report that spending time with the engaged or newly married couple helps them revive some of the romantic energy that brought them together in the first place. Talking and thinking about marriage and what makes it work—in order to be helpful to the younger couple—helps them too.[9]

Being "real" from the pulpit and in classroom situations about the challenges of being married can also help congregation members be more willing to tackle the problems in their own marriages. Some congregations have such an atmosphere of success and happiness that couples are motivated to cover over any problems. Facing problems rather than ignoring them will promote long-range marital health, and if the atmosphere in the congregation encourages some degree of honesty about problems in marriage, members will be more likely to seek help. Publishing a list of community resources such as counseling centers, Marriage Encounter dates, and marriage enrichment activities at other churches will also help people pay attention to their marriages.

As congregation leaders, we also need to remember that there are married couples of all ages who never had children. Some are battling infertility, and their monthly disappointment is deeply painful. Some have chosen not to have children and may experience irritation that there are those who view them as incomplete. We need to walk the delicate balance of affirming the reality of the challenges to a marriage that children can precipitate, while also encouraging couples without children to work hard on their marriages too.

Aging Parents

Steve's mother got cancer when Steve was in his early 40s. Steve's parents lived five hours away in the next state, and he got used to pounding the pavement to visit and support his parents during the long stage of chemotherapy.

During those months, Steve's father was a trooper. He took over domestic tasks he had never tackled before, and he tenderly cared for his wife as her energy drained away and then later returned. Her short-term memory seemed to be greatly affected by the chemotherapy, and he worked hard to compensate for her gentle air of distraction.

One day Steve got the call he was dreading. No, it wasn't his mother. To everyone's surprise, it was his father. He had died completely unexpectedly, sitting in his favorite armchair.

In the months that followed, Steve's mother's cancer went into remission. Steve tried to celebrate this good news in the midst of his grief about his father. To complicate matters further, Steve's mother's short-term memory did not return as her health returned. All of Steve's sisters are married with children, but Steve is single. He arranged to visit his mother every month to balance her checkbook and help her with doctor's appointments.

The one-year anniversary of Steve's father's death passed. His mother's memory continued to deteriorate. Was it Alzheimer's? The doctors weren't sure. Steve and his sisters became convinced their mother needed to live somewhere with more supervision and support. They found her a warm and comfortable retirement home, close to her friends and church. They cleaned out her house and put it on the market. Because Steve was the only one without a family, he made countless trips up and down the freeway.

Soon after the house was sold, the cancer came back. Steve's mother became weaker and needed more care than the retirement home provided. Steve and one of his sisters live in the same town, so they found a retirement home there and moved their mother. The next step was pneumonia. More care was needed. They found another retirement home that provided more nursing care.

Steve and his sisters are now facing difficult decisions about appropriate chemotherapy for their mother. The agony of the decisions is compounded by daily phone calls from their mother's closest friend, who is convinced that Steve's mother isn't getting appropriate medical treatment for her disease. The latest development is the threat of a lawsuit from this friend.

Steve finds himself vacillating between tears and anger almost every day. He is furious at his mother's friend. He also feels anger when he thinks about his mother's medical care. Surely the doctors could do more to help his mother. He feels so helpless in the face of his mother's needs. Is he doing enough? He longs for his mother to be comfortable, well fed, happy again. He finds himself clinging to his mother's life because he doesn't want to feel alone in the world.

"It's not what I expected," says Steve. "None of this is what I expected."

Maureen's concerns about her mother are completely different from Steve's. Maureen's mother is 70. Widowed five years ago, she is an active and energetic golfer and an enthusiastic gardener. For the past year, she has been dating a man her age. They have decided to live together rather than get married, because Maureen's mother's pension benefits through Maureen's father's job will cease if she gets married again.

Maureen has two children approaching adolescence. "How can I tell my kids that sex outside of marriage is wrong, when their own grandmother is doing it? I'm not a judgmental person and I don't need everyone in the world to do what I think is right, but this is their own grandmother who is living with someone outside of marriage. What in the world can I say? How can I possibly take the kids to visit her? In a sense I feel like I've lost my own mother."

Mitch, in his late 40s, has an equally difficult situation to deal with. His mother died. She had always been the one who took care of his father, who has a myriad of health problems. Mitch and his brother decided his father needed to be moved from his home halfway across the country to the town where they lived. They found him a spot in a nursing home.

But the adjustment to nursing home living has been very difficult. Mitch, his brother, and both of their wives take turns accompanying their father to meals because he doesn't like to go on his own. Mitch's father is bewildered, angry, and very irritable. Mitch and his brother have no idea how to help him adjust to his new setting. The situation is very difficult, but no one can think of anything better.

People in their midlife years often face complex, confusing, or just plain sad situations with their parents. Many people in their midlife years will lose one or both parents to death. For some, this will be their first encounter with the death of a loved one.

Others will experience a variety of difficult questions. How can I get my father to eat right, now that Mom is gone? He lives on crackers and cheese. What should I do about my mother who has a whole array of prescribed medications but has no idea why most of them were ordered by the doctor? Should I encourage my parents in their plan to sell the family house and move to Florida, or should I tell them forcefully that they will miss so many good years with their grandchildren if they do that? Now that my parents can't take care of their house, and I don't want to, how can I encourage them to sell it and move to some kind of retirement community? How can I get my parents to let go of my life and let me live it the way I want to? How can I stop them from meddling in the lives of my children?

Steve's experience of the unexpectedness of the whole situation is not unusual, nor are Mitch's confusion about how to help his father adjust to a new place or Maureen's frustration about her mother's choices. Many midlife folks will encounter unexpected and powerful emotions in the face of bewildering circumstances involving their parents.

Congregations can help by providing a listening ear to midlife children as they face issues with their parents that they never could have imagined. Establishing a Stephen ministry program and promoting small groups for folks at midlife are two ways to make sure people have a place to talk.

We can also provide help with grief even before it happens. If a congregation has in place a program of regular classes on the grief process, then people in the midlife years will know that resources will be available when they need them. Significant faith questions can be triggered by watching people suffer. Can I really believe God is good when I see my parents' endless medical problems? Can I believe God is good when I see one of my parents grieve so deeply when the partner dies? Can I believe God is good when I feel cast adrift in the world when I lose both parents? Some of these questions can be addressed proactively in sermons, newsletter articles, classes, and seminars. Practical help such as providing meals and helping with funeral services can communicate to the bereaved that someone cares in the midst of pain, and in addition, those who provide the help are prepared in a small way for the time they will have to face similar grief.

Special attention to grief issues should be considered for the holiday season. Grief can be most intense during the holidays. Mentioning this reality in a sermon, writing an article in the church newsletter, or offering a seminar on grief during the holidays can help people in pain.

One Unitarian Universalist minister has an idea worth considering. She offers a class to help people face the fear of death that is common to so many of us. She believes that part of why it is so hard to navigate the death of family members is that our grief is complicated by the fear of our own death. We can ignore that fear most of the time, but when we are faced with the serious illness or death of a family member, that fear comes to the surface and complicates everything we are feeling. Addressing that fear during ordinary times of life can help us prepare for the times of stress when we have to face the death of someone we love.

If we want our congregations to be sensitive to the needs of people at midlife, we will have to remember that they may be dealing with life-and-death issues in their own parents' lives. The confusion and lack of control may be very difficult, and we need to be sensitive to this reality.

A Variety of Family Patterns

There are many people in our congregations who won't fit into the patterns described in this chapter. We may have people who are newly single after a divorce, some of them feeling peace at last and others feeling terror about their futures. We may have new mothers in their 40s and new fathers in their 50s. We may have grandmothers in their late 30s. We may have all sorts of complicated blended families with a variety of needs. While some people are mourning the death of their parents, others will be mourning the death of a child.

We probably will have a large number of baffled parents of teenagers, along with significant numbers of single people who have never married. Some congregation members will be dealing with complex issues in their own parents' lives.

Many of these family situations at midlife involve joy and gladness, and we want to celebrate as a congregation with those who are rejoicing. Many of these family situations involve loss, and we need to think carefully about how to care for those who are experiencing loss of dreams, relationships, and roles.

Questions for Reflection

Questions for you to use personally in reflection, journaling, or discussion:

1. Which losses are most real to you at midlife? In what ways have you grieved those losses? In what ways have you tried to ignore or deny the reality of loss?

2. Which family issues are most real to you at midlife? What emotions are raised by your current stage in life? What faith questions are triggered? What kind of support have you received? What could you do to receive more support?

3. Which support systems have helped you cope with family issues at midlife? Pray some prayers of thankfulness for the people who have supported you. What kind of additional support would you like to have? What steps can you take to find that support?

Questions for congregational leaders:

1. List the ways your congregation currently ministers to people with regard to the more common family issues that emerge at midlife: singleness, parenting adolescents, marriage enrichment, supporting people with aging or dying parents. What ways does your congregation provide support for the many other family-related issues that are common during the midlife years, such as infertility, blended families, divorce, and parenting late in life? Evaluate the effectiveness of your existing support ministries. Spend some time praying prayers of thankfulness for the people who are served by these ministries.

2. Brainstorm new ways your congregation could provide support for people as they face the many family-related issues of midlife.

used by Paradoxes

For everything there is a season, and a time for every matter under heaven: . . . a time to weep, and a time to laugh; . . . a time to love, and a time to hate.

Ecclesiastes 3:1, 4, 8

"I laugh a lot more now," says Linda, 46. "I laugh at the absurdity of life. So many things seemed black and white in my 20s and 30s. Things were clear and obvious. I thought I knew a lot. Now there are still some things I'm certain about—like God's goodness and the centrality of love and grace—but I am also certain that life is full of mystery and ambiguity. I just don't know everything. No human being can see truth in every area all the time.

"Life has to have balance, and part of that balance is acknowledging that there are many good things in life, but most of them are good only at the right time. Work is good, but too much of it makes a person compulsive or exhausted or sick. Rest is good, but too much rest makes a person lazy or irresponsible. The key is keeping work and rest in some sort of tension, some sort of balance. There are lots of other areas that also seem some-what paradoxical. I have to laugh at the way life has turned out. In so many areas, it's not black and white anymore at all."

Linda is not alone in her experience of paradox and ambiguity at midlife. In many areas the wisdom of midlife embraces the balance of opposites. Many of us become aware at midlife that we are essentially alone as hu-man beings, that we are born alone and will face death alone, yet we are more aware than ever before of our interconnectedness with family, friends, neighbors, and coworkers. We learn to express love more passionately at the same time that we grow in assertiveness. We celebrate the joy of the physical creation and our physical bodies at the same time that we grow in understanding the ultimate significance of the spiritual reality that lies behind all of creation.

Understanding some of these paradoxes can help congregational leaders plan events and programs. Folks of all ages can benefit from the suggestions in this chapter. People at midlife and beyond may be hungry for a focus on these areas.

The Physical World: More and Less Significant

For many, the admonition "slow down and smell the roses" has particular impact at midlife. The physical world and all its beauties take on an increased role as balm for the soul and food for the spirit. In my 40s I have noticed that the spring flowers seem much more beautiful than they used to be. Each year I find myself asking, "Is spring more beautiful than usual this year? Or am I noticing it more?" Since I've had the same experience for several years in a row, I have to conclude that I'm the one who has changed, not the spring weather. More than ever before I am awed by the beauty God has placed in creation.

Many of the people I interviewed echoed these feelings, and, at the same time, they recounted the ways money and possessions have declined in significance as they journeyed through the midlife years. The physical world has become more and less important at the same time. Nature, beauty, and art take on an increased importance, while possessions, particularly for the sake of status or achievement, seem less important.

This development is consistent with the values of the great faith traditions: seeing the physical creation as a manifestation of the handiwork of God, seeing human artistic achievement as a reflection of God's image in humans, and keeping one's life free from the love of money and possessions. In our congregations we want to do everything possible to nurture this movement, particularly because we live in such a materialistic and acquisitive culture. Sometimes it seems that everything in the media encourages us to believe that more possessions are always better, and that we will be happier, sexier, and more fulfilled people if each of us simply buys one more thing.

Congregations can encourage movement towards simple living by sponsoring seminars or classes on simplicity. Even more effective are simplicity circles, where people band together to support each other as they make attempts to live more simply and to withstand the onslaughts of the media culture.

"The materialism of our culture is overwhelming," says Burt, 52. "We need all the help we can get to resist falling into the belief that more is always better. I have found support through participating in a simplicity circle. We gather together with the purpose of supporting each other as we try to live simple lives in this materialistic culture. We explore things like organic gardening, alternative means of transportation, shopping for things that don't damage the earth, ways to recycle what we have rather than buy something new. I have felt very supported."

Idea for congregations:
Form simplicity circles to provide support for simple living in our materialistic culture.

Exposure to the needs of the developing world can go a long way towards helping people put their possessions and money into perspective. The needs of people in the developing world can be presented to a congregation in a variety of ways, such as speakers, displays, fund-raising efforts, and articles in the newsletter. Trips to visit other countries are the most effective tactic, particularly when the trip involves some kind of service.

Several years ago at my own church, we offered a four-week class on money, with the goal of presenting the wide variety of material on money in the Old and New Testaments. It was one of the best-attended classes we have ever offered. We were amazed at the hunger in so many people to talk about money more openly. The class was structured with a lecture, followed by small-group discussions. Several participants told me that the discussions were eye-opening to them. They knew they struggled with money and all its power in their lives; before the class they had no idea that others struggled as well. Money is surrounded by a shroud of silence in so many settings.

Embracing the beauty of creation in our congregational ministries takes some creative thinking, because most of us experience the physical beauty of the world in the context of being outdoors, not being inside a building. Certainly the beauty of the physical world can be brought inside through the use of flowers and other natural decorations and by the effective use of windows.

Congregations can offer activities for groups that involve getting outside: a congregational bike trip, hike, bird-watching expedition, or camping trip. One congregation in Seattle holds its summer services outside on the lawn when weather permits.

For many people, art reflects the beauty of the physical world. One congregation has an arrangement with a nearby art gallery to display art inside the church building. When I visited there, I was transfixed by a display of small art quilts with all sorts of beautiful beading and stitching. Certainly those quilts reflected the intricacy of the world created by God.

For some, learning about science helps them appreciate the complexity of the created world. A lecture series about scientific discoveries would be unusual in many congregations, but it might help members connect with the physical world in a new way.

Rabbi James Mirel and psychotherapist Karen Bonnel Werth, in their book *Stepping Stones to Jewish Spiritual Living,*[1] recommend meditation on breath and on light to begin each day. These meditations, which have strong parallels in Christian tradition, are a way of slowing down and focusing on our present physical reality as a gift from God. Through focusing on our breath, we can affirm that just like air, God is present all around us and inside us. Through focusing on light, we affirm the way that God illumines all of life. Mirel and Werth suggest that by focusing on breath and light each morning, we remember that we—along with the whole creation—are sustained by God as we go into the day.

The Jewish tradition also helps us understand the significance of food as a connection between God and the created world. The special foods of Passover communicate truths about the history of God's interaction with the people of Israel, and that communication comes in a tactile, multi-sensory fashion. At Purim, special cookies are baked in the shape of Haman's hat in order to remind us of the story of the good queen Esther and the evil Haman who tried to destroy the people of Israel.

The festival of Succoth, in the fall, calls for a shelter to be built outside in memory of the Jews living in tents in the wilderness. Families spend as much time as possible outside in the shelter. Those of us who are not Jewish would do well to brainstorm ways we could act out our faith history in multisensory ways that connect us with God's creation.

Our Physical Bodies

For many, our physical bodies during the midlife years become more important and less important simultaneously. For some people who have been too busy in early adulthood to "slow down and smell the roses," they find great joy at midlife in discovering that their physical bodies can be a source of joy and an arena for connection with God. At the same time, the aches and pains of an aging body and the irritation of losing our looks—and maybe our hair—can give us a new level of detachment about the importance of the way we look.

Ken, 53, is a dentist. He has watched quite a few colleagues leave his profession because of back problems. At 50, he suffered his first twinges of back pain. After seeing a chiropractor a few times, he began a regimen of daily stretches. He realized that without some intentional effort, he could no longer count on his body to function efficiently like it did in his 20s and 30s.

Ken had always been physically active, biking a lot and walking with his wife. At 51, he began to use a cross-country ski machine, followed by lifting weights. He has gained muscle strength and takes great pleasure in admiring the muscles he has developed. He has the sense that he will be able to work for another decade at least, and he enjoys the feeling that his body is more consistent with the way God created him.

Several people talked to me about the joy of taking up yoga or various kinds of dance during the midlife years. They seemed to have arrived at a kind of revelation about their physical bodies, coming to the place of affirming the significance of spending consistent time and effort in order to nurture physical health by keeping their bodies strong and flexible.

Congregations can nurture this connection with the physical body in a number of ways. They can allow their space to be used for yoga or other exercise classes. They can encourage congregational fellowship activities that include a physical component, such as line dancing or contra dancing, bike rides, or hikes.

One church holds a health fair twice each year on Sunday mornings between and after the services. Community organizations are invited to participate, so that congregation members can get screening for blood pressure and cholesterol. All sorts of healthy recreational activities are promoted, and nurses and doctors are available to answer questions.

In that church, the health fair is organized by the parish nurse. She is a nurse who works part-time in a hospital and part-time in the congregation. Her job description involves nurturing all kinds of activities that promote health, both physical and emotional.

"We recently had a sermon on sex," says Bill. "And we have sermons on being generous with money and pledging to the congregation. But when is someone going to tackle the real issue: the power of money in our lives? At midlife I'm realizing all the ways I compromise my values for the sake of financial security. Everything in our culture tells us that money is of paramount importance. How can we resist that message? I would like to discuss this issue with others who have some of the same concerns."

Idea for congregations:
Offer a seminar, class, or sermon on money and its power in our lives.

The parish nurse in that congregation is also involved in helping to coordinate a monthly healing service. The presence of the nurse in that congregation, with all the resulting activities like the health fairs and the healing services, affirms human beings in their wholeness. Our physical, emotional, spiritual, and relational dimensions are connected.

Many churches are offering an interesting weight-loss program called Weigh Down. Operating from a conservative Christian viewpoint, the program stresses learning to listen to your body and its appetite. Gwen Shamblin, the founder, believes that many compulsive eaters have confused "heart hunger" with "stomach hunger." When we are lonely, sad, or discouraged, we feed those feelings with food, rather than eating only when our body is actually in need of fuel.[2]

Shamblin believes that the way we eat has profound implications for our faith. God made our bodies and created our appetite to help us know how to eat. Many people are in a kind of bondage to self-hate because of their eating habits and their weight. She longs to see people return to the God-given pattern of truly learning to listen to our appetite and eat accordingly. She also desires that people take their heart needs to God, who alone can meet those deepest longings.

While congregations sponsor activities that can promote a healthy relationship with our physical bodies and encourage physical health, they also need to stand firmly against our culture's preoccupation with appearance. Simplicity circles can provide support as people strive to stay free from our culture's obsessions. Small groups in homes, women's and men's groups, and discussion in classes and seminars can provide other places for people to discuss the ways we are called to live separate from these unhealthy forces in our society.

The book *Reviving Ophelia: Saving the Lives of Adolescent Girls*[3] had a profound impact on me. The author, psychologist Mary Pipher, argues that more and more adolescent girls are prey to depression, eating disorders, addictions, and suicide because of our look-obsessed, media-saturated culture. She coins the word "lookism" to describe our culture's obsession with appearance, which impacts teenage girls in such devastating ways.

As I read the book, I was overcome with emotions about my own teenage years and the pressure I felt to be beautiful. The book provided a deeply moving opportunity for "life review," to consider the impact of my childhood on my life today. The book could be used effectively in a seminar or class for parents of girls in the age range of eight to 14. The parents would gain an understanding of the forces at work in their daughters' lives, and, in addition, the parents would have the opportunity to explore the pressures they themselves have felt, and may continue to feel, to conform to society's standards in the area of physical appearance.

We cannot underestimate the power of advertisements, TV shows, and movies that promote the view that thin, beautiful, sexy bodies will make people happy. Our teenagers and children are not the only ones affected. We must be vocal about the limitations of our culture's view of happiness.

Work and Rest

The age range that we are considering in this book—35 to 55— encompasses huge changes in the area of career and work for many people. In that age range, a good number of women and a few men who have stayed home with children will go back to work. Others who have struggled to balance the needs of children while working part-time will gain the freedom to focus on their careers. Lots of people lose their jobs for various reasons during those years. Some folks make career changes that require a stint back in community college or university.

Mark, 45, works as a manager in city government. He says, "My midlife crisis began in my late thirties. It hit me big-time. I was asking all kinds of questions about my purpose in life, why I do what I do. At various times in my life I felt called to be a pastor, a teacher in a church setting, or a writer. Never an administrator!" Mark began to articulate a vision for his job that included providing loving care for the employees working under him. Essentially, he redefined the purpose of his job to put relationships at the center, which fits with his sense of call to be a pastor. In addition, he wrote a biography of his mother and is planning another writing project. Mark kept his job with the city, and he has much more peace about it now. His job redefinition and his weekend writing projects have enabled him to experience joy in his life again.

Idea for congregations:
Offer a class, seminar, or panel discussion on work. It could include personal stories or cover a theology of work, but be sure to include time for people to discuss or write about their personal vision for their work.

During the midlife years some people begin a career that feels like it is their life's work, while others retire. Some people stay in the same job throughout the age range of 35 to 55; some of them are content, challenged, and fulfilled, and others are living lives of quiet desperation. Some people leave salaried jobs to pursue the dream of owning their own business, while others close their business to return to the relative peace of being salaried employees.

Since there are so many diverse work experiences in this age range, can congregations hope to help in any way at all? Should they try to help?

I long for pastors, rabbis, and congregational leaders to act and talk in ways that affirm the significance of the number of hours people spend at work. In most congregations, work is a topic that is ignored, yet most congregation members spend more time working than doing anything else.

Most people living in the Western world have been deeply impacted by the Protestant work ethic. Congregations can help their members by promoting discussion about the implications of this work ethic today: In what ways is it healthy? Harmful? In what ways does it reflect our current priorities for work and rest?

Then there are other questions: Why do we work? Is it simply to put food on the table or is it connected to some innate part of human nature created by God? In what ways does our work connect us to God? How can people find meaning in their work?

All of these questions can be discussed in sermons, seminars, and classes. One person told me that he wrote a mission statement regarding his work, and it was a transforming experience to articulate his God-given purpose in working. A seminar or class could offer participants the opportunity to write their own personal mission statements regarding work.

One congregation held a work fair. People of different professions were asked to sit at booths and talk with congregation members as they came by. The intent was to provide a resource for youth and young adults and maybe for the occasional person over 30 who was considering changing jobs. Organizers of the fair were surprised at the number of adults of all ages who simply enjoyed talking with others about the pros and cons of their work. The fair started a dialog on the meaning of work that has continued.

Ken, mentioned above, realized around age 50 that if he wanted to keep working as a dentist for another decade, he would have to be intentional about keeping his body in shape. During the midlife years, many folks also experience the need to be more intentional about rest, realizing that they simply can't take for granted any longer their body and soul's ability to recover instantly from stress and hard work.

As baby boomers have entered midlife, many have discovered the benefits of observing a weekly Sabbath. I have seen articles on Sabbath observance in airplane magazines and local newspapers as well as in religious publications. Jews, Christians, and folks with no particular faith commitment are realizing the ancient wisdom of taking a break each week.

In his science fiction novel *Perelandra*, C. S. Lewis presents a number of paradoxes in a long speech by the gods who rule our solar system. One of Lewis's paradoxes is the fact that we are "infinitely necessary," because God's love needs a channel to flow in, while at the same time we are "infinitely superfluous," because God's love comes from God's bounty, not from our need or our worth.[4]

My husband and I have been dedicated Sabbath observers ever since we spent 18 months living in Israel 20 years ago. We experienced the peace of having one day each week without shopping, public transport, restaurants, or movies. We have chosen to observe a weekly Sabbath—and the day of the week varies based on our work schedules—so that each week we can experience the reality of being infinitely superfluous. The world goes on without us quite efficiently while we are taking our weekly break. Six days each week we act on the truth that we are infinitely necessary, because God is working through us to repair and redeem the world. One day each week we stop to remember that we are superfluous; God is God and we are not.

The form of the Sabbath varies from one person to the next. Some consider the Sabbath a time to encourage family togetherness. Others, like my husband and I, center their Sabbath around doing nothing productive. Some find it most restful to take a Sabbath from our culture, so they spend one 24-hour period each week without newspapers, TV, radio, or shopping. The Hebrew word for Sabbath means "stop." In the fast pace of our culture, stopping once a week, no matter what form it takes, is a good idea.

Protestant churches are the greatest offenders at not encouraging rest. Many strands of Christianity affirm that the need to obey the Sabbath laws ended with the death of Christ. In addition, the Protestant work ethic has so permeated our congregations that we tend to believe that work is always better than anything else.

When my husband and I lived in Israel, we experienced the Sabbath as a gift, not as an onerous commandment. When we got back to the United States, we were amazed that most people were totally uninterested in hearing about the weekly rhythm we had enjoyed so much. In the 20 years since we returned from Israel, we have been delighted to watch the growing interest in Sabbath observance coming from so many different sources.

On the one hand, promoting Sabbath observance in congregations is fairly straightforward. All of these can be helpful: articles in the newsletter, sermons on rest and on the Sabbath, or a seminar for families on creative ways to engage children in a special Sabbath meal.

On the other hand, the issue of rest and Sabbath observance is very complex. Do the pastors and rabbis in your congregation ever rest? Do they provide a model of human beings who live with a healthy rhythm of work and rest? Are there lay leaders in your congregation who are compulsive about serving and find it impossible to say no? Do you have the habit of scheduling committee meetings on the same day as your worship services? All of these questions need to be addressed.

In this era of extremely busy people, congregational leaders face the very significant issue of helping people find space for God. People in the midlife years are some of the busiest people around. At the same time that we endeavor to encourage healthy attitudes towards work, we also need to promote patterns of rest that make space for God to break into our lives.

"I've been doing clerical work all my life," says Jean, 43. "I wanted to go to college, but some things happened and I ended up working instead. I don't want to spend the rest of my life typing letters for other people. I want to find a job where I can work at my own initiative. I'd like to work in some kind of service or ministry. But I have no idea what my strengths or gifts are. I don't have any idea what I could offer in a job or in some area of service, except clerical tasks, and I don't want to do that."

Idea for congregations:
Offer a class or seminar on exploring spiritual gifts and/or personality type to help people explore their strengths and gifts.

Freedom and Discipline

Merrill, 46, and Tom, 42, are old friends. Merrill has been disappointed in recent years that Tom has virtually stopped attending church. Tom joined a bike club and spends a lot of Sunday mornings on long bike trips. When he's not biking, he enjoys having a relaxed Sunday morning at home.

One day Merrill and Tom were talking about midlife issues. Merrill said, "For me, the discipline of attending church and trying to be a faithful Christian has been an anchor in the midlife years. You know how tough it's been with our kids. The teenage years raised one issue after another. Going to church helped calm me down and get centered on Christ once again."

Tom replied, "I used to feel that way about church. Now I experience God most vividly in the wind and sun when I'm biking."

"But what about your kids?" Merrill asked. "Don't you want them to grow up with the habit of attending church?"

"Sarah takes them sometimes. I believe they need the freedom to decide for themselves what they want to do about their beliefs."

"They're too young for that! I think you're robbing them of the habit of faithful church attendance that can last a lifetime," Merrill said. "Church is an anchor for me. If I hadn't been attending all my life, if I didn't have the habit of attendance, I'm not sure I would be able to draw such strength from it now. I think you're doing your children a disservice. Plus, I'm worried about you."

"I'm fine. I feel as close to God as I ever did. Lay off," Tom replied.

I find in myself bits and pieces of both Tom and Merrill. At midlife I have gained a stronger sense of freedom from the "shoulds" and "oughts" that seemed to characterize my early adulthood. I find God in all sorts of unexpected places. Yet at the same time, I am deeply grateful for the faith habits of a lifetime. Church attendance truly is an anchor for me. I worry about friends who have drifted away from church in their midlife years.

The popularity of Celtic and Benedictine spirituality in Christian congregations illustrates the hunger for structure and discipline coupled with freedom. Kathleen Norris, a poet and a Presbyterian, has written several books in which she discusses her involvement with a nearby Benedictine monastery. Her book *The Cloister Walk* describes the church year as she has observed it in her many visits to the monastery. The structure of the church year provides a framework for exploring many different aspects of faith. The freedom to explore ideas is coupled with a structure—the yearly Christian calendar—that has endured for 2,000 years.

Celtic spirituality also provides a challenge to embrace both freedom and discipline. The Celts sensed the presence of God in all of life. They loved nature. The Christian Celts looked for God both in church and in everyday life. Yet discipline was woven into this free-flowing expectation of the presence of God in all of life. Celts loved pilgrimages, and the commitment of time and resources required for a spiritual journey was expected to bear much fruit. They embraced faithful friendships—"soul friends"—and expected that faithfulness in friendships would require costly discipline at the same time that it brought great joy and love.[5]

In this age of cafeteria religion, when cultural forces are encouraging our congregational members to pick and choose the aspects they like from different faith traditions and even from different religions, we can unashamedly assert the benefits of discipline in observing long-standing faith traditions. I enjoy taking groups of women from my church to stay at a Benedictine monastery. The sisters at the monastery live in an aura of peace that is palpable. Their submission to the disciplines of their order—prayer, service, and hospitality—clearly gives them something we all long for.

Whatever disciplines we choose to promote in our congregations—a daily prayer/meditation time, consistent attendance at worship, regular study of Scripture, ongoing participation in service—we need not fear that we are calling people to something irrelevant or unnecessary. Spiritual hunger in our culture, and even in our congregations, is real. Freedom and discipline must be explored in tension now more than ever. We need to affirm both.

Independence and Interdependence

"I spent my 20s and 30s jumping through other people's hoops," says Ted, 52. "When I was in college and graduate school, I worked hard to fulfill my professors' expectations. Then I went into teaching. More hoops. I carefully and faithfully jumped through them all.

"I have always been very sensitive to the people around me, and I spent those years in the first half of adulthood trying to please all the people around me all of the time. I find I just can't do it any more. If success means jumping through more hoops and pleasing more people, I guess I just won't be successful any more."

Ted's "declaration of independence" has been a healthy step for him. It has helped him gain some appropriate dispassionate distance from his teenage children. It has helped him speak more clearly to his coworkers and his wife when something is important to him.

Many people, particularly women, told me in interviews that during the midlife years they have grown in the ability to know what they want and how to ask for it in a straightforward manner. People who have the tendency to be very sensitive to the needs and opinions of those around them will never turn into hard-driving, totally self-directed folks. However, during the midlife years many of them will grow in the ability to ask in a clear and direct manner for what they need and want.

This is a significant step of growth. As I talk with friends and parishioners who are struggling in their marriages, I observe that in at least half of the cases, the wife has a very hard time articulating clearly what she needs and wants. She wants to please her husband and her children; unfortunately, over the years her own voice has been lost. Finding her voice—and speaking clearly—is an essential step.

Many of our congregations are infected by the number of parishioners working hard to care for everyone around them and striving to be "nice." Certainly we are called to be servants to one another. Christians in particular take their model from Jesus, who emptied himself for the sake of others. When I meet people who struggle with their powerful drive to constantly please the people around them, I always recommend a careful study of the Gospels. Jesus was certainly sensitive to the people around him, but he was also one of the most self-directed and assertive individuals ever portrayed in literature.

The word "assertive" has taken on a negative connotation and is often confused with "aggressive." Aggression involves hostility and conveys the flavor of an attack. Many people who have been very caring and loving reach the ends of their ropes and become aggressive. When they express their own needs, they can fall easily into aggression. Behind their statement of need or desires lies the thought that they have been caring for others; why haven't these others been caring for them? The hostile implication is that the people around them haven't been loving them enough.

Assertiveness, on the other hand, involves a simple declaration of need, intent, or desire. There is no hostility involved. There is no sense that "you should have known what I needed," or "how could you have missed my signals that I want something?" Assertiveness is straightforward, clear, and nonjudgmental.

Ironically, assertiveness enables connectedness. In fact, being able to ask in a straightforward way for what we want and need enables relational connection better than a constant striving to do what other people want. The central issue is honesty.

Ted reflects on the way his growing assertiveness has impacted his relationships. "Having a voice and stating my needs clearly is important in having an honest relationship with someone. If I'm going to have a relationship, I want to be me. I've been surprised that being more honest helps build my self-esteem. I feel better when I'm being me. And when I'm being me, my self-esteem grows."

Ted has noticed a change in his confidence about his own views. "I do have a lot to say," he notes. "My views often are right. I don't always have to seek others' opinions. I've had enough life experience that I now trust my own intuition. Before, I didn't have enough experience, so I didn't trust my own viewpoint."

Midlife expert Gail Sheehy recommends that men in their 40s spend time and energy consciously nurturing relationships.[6] Tom experiences that need. He says, "I yearn for more relationships. I yearn to have more intimate connections with men, where we can speak about deeper things. I don't have it as much as I'd like yet, but I do have it with one of my grown sons and one of my cousins. That's more than I used to have, and I'm very grateful."

Women also experience more contentedness in their marriages, in their friendships, and at work as they grow in being honest and expressing their wants, needs, and viewpoints honestly. Interconnectedness can be nurtured as we grow in healthy independence.

Congregations can enable this growth in independence and interconnectedness by encouraging honesty and by affirming the reality of conflict. This can be accomplished by affirming from the pulpit that "niceness" isn't always the best idea, particularly when it covers over honesty. We can affirm that caring and love go hand-in-hand with honest expression of personal beliefs, desires, and needs.

Classes and seminars could cover topics such as healthy assertiveness and conflict management. Small groups are an excellent arena for learning to express honest needs while also growing in ability to depend on others and be intimate with others.

Pastors and other trained congregational leaders can make themselves available to visit small groups to help with conflict situations. This encourages people to understand that relationships and honesty are both important, and that conflict can be an avenue for growth in both.

A Variety of Paradoxes

We have looked at several paradoxes that people often experience in the midlife years. There are many others. Many people find themselves becoming more flexible and open in lots of areas while they become more convinced of the truth of a few of their convictions. Flexibility and certainty seem to come simultaneously at midlife.

Some people experience more joy in their work as they place less of their identity in it. Some people experience more joy in their marriage as they place less of their identity in it. Some people hate divorce in principle yet find that their divorce was a significant growth stage for them. Some people stay married out of duty, expecting to experience drudgery, and then are surprised to find that love returns.

Midlife is a life stage of rueful shaking of the head. So many things are different than they seemed. So many things are confusing yet wonderful. So many things are important, yet difficult to understand. It's great to be alive, we realize, but life certainly is surprising sometimes.

Questions for Reflection

Questions for you to use personally in reflection, journaling, or discussion:

1. In what ways have the paradoxes described in this chapter impacted your life:

    - the importance and irrelevance of the physical world
    - the importance and irrelevance of your body
    - work and rest
    - freedom and discipline
    - independence and interdependence

2. How have you responded to these paradoxes? How would you like to respond? With what new patterns of behavior or thought would you like to experiment?

Questions for congregational leaders:

1. In what ways could your congregation do more to affirm the significance of the physical world as God's creation? Could you sponsor any activities that get people outside together? Could you use art in your building? Could you create arenas to discuss money, simplicity, the needs of the developing world, and the materialism of our culture?

2. In what ways could your congregation affirm the significance of our

physical bodies? In what ways does your congregation separate spirituality from the physical world, particularly the physical body?

3. In what ways does your congregation promote healthy attitudes to-
    wards work and rest? What could you do to provide arenas where
    people can discuss their work? What could you do to encourage your
    pastors and church leaders to rest? In what ways could you explore
    and promote Sabbath-keeping?

4. In what ways could your congregational leaders promote the necessity
    of discipline in spiritual growth, while balancing it with a commensurate
    attitude that embraces freedom? What are the arenas in your congre-
    gation where freedom and discipline are both embraced? How could
    you increase those opportunities?

5. In what ways is your congregation infected with an overemphasis on
    "niceness"? In what ways could your congregational leaders communi-
    cate that they value honesty? Could you offer an assertiveness training
    course? A course on conflict management? How could you increase
    the number of entry points where people can begin to connect with
    each other?

CHAPTER 5

The Golden Riches of the Shadow

Even the darkness is not dark to you; the night is as bright as the day, for darkness is as light to you.

Psalm 139:12

At 26, Sarah married a man with custody of his two children. She and her husband later had two children of their own.

When Sarah turned 40, the older kids were almost out of the nest and the younger two were in school. Sarah realized she was angry. Very, very angry. So angry that she sometimes felt like killing her husband or her stepchildren.

For 14 years Sarah had been an attentive wife and a supportive stepmother. As her own children came along, she had added the responsibilities of caring for two more children. She had tried her hardest to be faithful to everyone and to do a good job. Sarah is innately conscientious, dependable, and reliable, and those character traits were manifested every day of those 14 years.

So, Sarah asked herself, where was this anger coming from? There had been some problems with her husband's ex-wife, which had caused frustrations in the management of her stepchildren, but those had largely passed. She and her husband had a friendly marriage characterized by partnership and good communication. They frequently had date nights and laughed a lot together.

The anger seemed out of proportion to the irritations Sarah experienced. Sarah couldn't figure out what was going on. Sarah didn't know she was meeting her shadow, which was emerging from her unconscious mind to make itself known.

Bernie was also encountering his shadow, and he also was unaware of it. At 50, Bernie noticed all kinds of changes in his body that were very frustrating to him. He used to enjoy throwing a baseball around with his two sons, but now his sons had moved on to college level baseball, and they could throw much harder than Bernie could. He couldn't jog with his sons any longer either. As they became accomplished athletes, their idea of jogging was to run up and down hills that completely defeated Bernie.

Bernie's hair was almost completely gray, and it was noticeably thin on top. Bernie religiously applied Rogaine every morning and evening, and he observed a slight thickening of his hair, but the thin patch still seemed to be enormously unattractive. Every time Bernie passed a mirror, he noticed his hair. The ugliness of his hair jumped out at him. He despised everything about his hair: the steel-gray color, the thin patches, its wispy texture even where it was still thick.

His hair seemed to represent everything he hated about getting old. His hair indicated to him that he was no longer attractive to women, although his wife told him frequently that she loved him. His hair told him he was no longer a real man, which was made clear to him every time he couldn't keep up with his sons in the athletic arena. His wife pointed out to him that he was remarkably fit for a fifty-year-old. Her words had no impact.

Bernie's gray and thinning hair seemed to tell to him that he was also losing competence. His company had gone through several periods of downsizing in recent years, and it was true that Bernie had kept his job, but he was always worried that he would be next to get a pink slip.

What Is the Shadow?

The shadow is all the elements of our inner self—feelings, emotions, ideas, and beliefs—with which we cannot identify and which are repressed because of our values, our culture, or our education, that is, everything we have learned in every setting of our lives.

The concept of the shadow originated in the work of Carl Jung, and many other authors have developed the concept further. Best-selling author Robert Bly describes the shadow as "the long bag we drag behind us." He believes that when we were children we had a personality that we could describe as having 360 degrees. Energy came from all parts of ourselves in all directions. Then, one day we noticed our parents didn't like some of the energy we radiated. Bly writes that our parents "said things like, 'Can't you be still?' Or 'It isn't nice to try to kill your brother.' Behind us we have an invisible bag, and the part of us our parents don't like, we, to keep our parents' love, put in the bag."

Later, Bly continues, "our teachers have their say: 'Good children don't get angry over such little things.' So we take our anger and put it in the bag." He reflects, "By the time my brother and I were twelve in Madison, Minnesota, we were known as 'the nice Bly boys.' Our bags were already a mile long."[1]

In high school our peers influence us as much as our parents and our teachers. We disown parts of our inner selves because of the demands of the fashion industry and the influence of television and movie stars. All around us, voices are telling us what is appropriate and what is not appropriate, and we respond by cutting off parts of our personality and identity. We are right to reject certain parts of ourselves: our desire to hurt others or our desire to solve problems by using violence. But some of the rejected parts of ourselves are full of potential and promise. We all have hidden gifts and abilities that have never had the chance to grow and develop because we felt we couldn't acknowledge that part of ourselves.

One woman never took any initiative to develop her ability in mathematics because her family wanted her to be a pretty secretary or kindergarten teacher. A man who is innately very gentle and caring worked hard to develop professional skills because of our culture's pressure. The mathematical abilities and the gentle, caring heart stay buried in the shadow until something triggers their emergence.

Bly believes that we put things in the long bag—our shadow—until we are about 20, then we spend the rest of our lives getting them out. Many others who write about the shadow believe that we continue to put things into our shadow until midlife, and that one of the tasks of the second half of life is to unpack the bag, bit by bit.

Two writers on midlife, Janice Brewi and Anne Brennan, believe that "the first half of life is, as it were, for the growth and differentiation of the Shadow. The whole second half of life is for the greater and greater integration of the Shadow."[2] The word "integration" helps us chart an agenda for facing the material in our shadow. Our goal is to grow in understanding what is there and to integrate it into our lives.

This bag we drag behind us contains a variety of elements of ourselves. Evil is there. Undeveloped skills and potentials are there. Emotions that were considered inappropriate in our families are there. For instance, some families allow the expression of anger or aggression, but most do not. Some families allow vulnerability, sexuality, and strong emotions to be expressed, but many do not. Some families allow artistic expression, intellectual development, or financial ambition to be expressed, but some do not. Any of these elements of our personalities may have been put into our shadow because we knew we would get along better in our families and with our friends if we didn't manifest them.

In the remainder of this chapter, we will explore the contents of the shadow and then look at the ways we can deal with its emergence.

Darkness and Evil

When one of my sons was in elementary school, he often talked about killing people. These conversations took place in the context of his anger about things that he didn't like. He always felt that killing the offender was the right response to any kind of violation of his will.

Sometimes I handled these discussions somewhat effectively, saying, "I can see you are very angry. I can understand that you're so angry you think Timmy should die. Of course, I want to affirm that it is never appropriate to kill someone because you're angry."

Other times I just got irritated, because these conversations seemed to happen too often for my taste. Whether I handled these conversations well or poorly, the net effect was that my son put his desire to kill into his shadow. And that is completely appropriate. Part of the process of growing up is to set aside those behaviors that we cannot afford to express because we live in community.

According to the experts on the shadow, we live the first half of our adult lives in ignorance of most of its contents. By midlife, we are beginning to discover what is there. The desire to kill when we are angry is there in the shadow for most of us. We will probably be surprised, maybe humiliated and angry, to find it there.

Sarah, the stepmother who would sometimes like to kill her husband and her stepchildren, is not alone. Many of us find ourselves at midlife facing darkness and evil inside us that has been hidden away for years. We may find ourselves cheating on our taxes in a small but disgusting way. We may find ourselves doing mean-spirited things we can't explain rationally.

We are forced to face, at least to some extent, the fact that we aren't really the nice people we thought we were.

We may also find a powerful drive to addiction as the contents of our shadow make themselves known. These addictive urges emerge at midlife when we realize that our "small" addictions—to coffee or chocolate for example—mask a part of our very being that craves instant fulfillment and constant gratification. We may find ourselves acknowledging that our patterns of shopping or our habits of thinking about sex really add up to a kind of addiction that is doing us no good at all.

This acknowledgement of our potential for evil is a very healthy step of growth. It reduces the arrogance that often characterizes people in the first half of adulthood. It creates compassion for people in need, because we recognize that we are capable of almost any kind of self-destructive or violent behavior.

We may find ourselves motivated to become involved in caring for prisoners, because we realize that we have the potential to rob and kill people. We are grateful that we never acted on that potential, and we have compassion for those who did.

We may find joy in serving homeless people, because we recognize that if our own addictive behaviors had taken a slightly different form, we could have been the kind of chronic addicts that end up homeless. We may find ourselves listening more gently to the struggles of family members or congregation members who used to drive us crazy because we realize that deep inside, we are just as messed up as we always thought they were.

Both in private pastoral relationships and in public worship settings, congregational leaders need to give people the freedom to express or acknowledge the horrors they may be finding inside themselves. This will happen only as we who are congregational leaders become more honest about our own potential for evil.

In so many communities of faith, a mask of niceness is valued very highly. Obviously, we need to affirm the value of loving and kind behavior. However, in addition, we need to affirm that self-destructive desires lie close below the surface for most of us. An atmosphere among congregational leaders that affirms some degree of personal honesty will bear good fruit. Hypocrisy will be reduced, people will be affirmed in their midlife journeys, and everyone will have the opportunity to grow in that most wonderful character trait, compassion.

Emotions

Little Samantha is a passionate child with great highs and lows. Her mother, who is blessed with a much more serene temperament, can't understand the intensity of Samantha's emotions.

"I hate Jessica!" Samantha shouts. "She never shares! I gave her half of my cookies yesterday, but she wouldn't give me any of hers today. And she had really cool Christmas cookies with sprinkles! I hate her."

"Oh, Samantha," her mother sighs. "Don't be so angry. We can make Christmas cookies with sprinkles. Come on. Let's check in the cupboard to see if we have any sprinkles in Christmas colors."

Samantha can see the tired expression on her mother's face, and Samantha can hear the tired tone in her mother's voice. Once again, her mother has communicated to Samantha that anger is an unacceptable emotion. So Samantha stuffs her anger into her shadow.

Anger

Many people in communities of faith were raised to believe that anger is always evil or wrong. Yet anger is simply an emotion. Because it is an emotion, it is neutral; anger is neither good nor evil. In her book *Anger: The Misunderstood Emotion*,[3] psychologist Carol Tavris points out that anger helps us understand what is important to us. It was anger against the injustice of slavery that fueled the anti-slavery movement. It is anger against domestic violence that has empowered so many communities to provide safe houses for wives and children in danger.

Think about Mothers Against Drunk Driving. It was founded by a mother who was angry about the death of her child at the hands of a drunk driver. The very acronym, MADD, expresses anger. We need to remember that anger at injustice is one of the most compelling forces empowering us to act for justice in the world.

On the much smaller scale of everyday life, anger again helps us understand what is important to us. Appropriate examination of our small-scale anger may motivate us to exercise, eat better, act kindly to our children, or maybe clean out the drawers of our desk. On a day-to-day basis, our anger provides motivation for all kinds of desirable behavior as we understand how we want things to be different.

Accessing anger at midlife is essential, because one of the tasks of midlife is to figure out what is important to us. The stepmother, Sarah, described at the beginning of the chapter, is finding that her anger reveals that she is very tired of totally submerging her desires and priorities in serving her family. Yet she doesn't really know what her desires and priorities are. Her anger will help her figure them out.

When we find ourselves angry about something at work, we can ask ourselves what we care about so passionately. When we talk with someone who is expressing anger, we can encourage them to go deeper to access the inner values that have been violated.

Our congregations are filled with people who are afraid of expressing anger because they were raised in a time when anger was not validated, and they were raised in families in which anger was not affirmed in any way as a positive source of energy or information. Many people in our congregations will begin to experience anger at midlife as the contents of the shadow emerge.

Anger in itself is simply an emotion that gives us information about what we care about. Anger can motivate us to work for justice. But anger can also motivate us to rape, kill, and destroy human life. How we respond when we are angry moves us into arenas of right and wrong.

At midlife, a kind and warm person may suddenly become passionate, even strident, about the rights of homosexual people. Others may become fiery, single-issue advocates for any one of a huge number of causes. Others may experience powerful anger at their spouse, children, siblings, parents, friends, coworkers, or neighbors.

In our congregations we need to affirm the place of anger in the great social movements of human history. We need to affirm that anger is a good source of information, and that we enter into the arena of right and wrong only when we begin to act on our anger. We need to talk about anger—in sermons, classes, and seminars—in ways that will free people to explore the role of anger in their lives. We need to provide practical help, such as information or training about ways to express anger appropriately, in order to help people face this powerful emotion in a healthy way.

Fear

Fear is another emotion, similar to anger, that is neutral when we experience it. Just like anger, fear can motivate us to appropriate action. It is my fear of car accidents that motivates me to drive carefully. My fear of earthquakes motivates me to take some measures to earthquake-proof my house. These are appropriate reactions to fear.

Fear can also motivate us toward counterproductive behavior such as avoidance of truth telling and unhealthy nonengagement in life. Fear can become irrational and obsessive, resulting in terror and excessive passivity.

Bernie, the man mentioned at the beginning of the chapter, is facing a lot of fears at midlife. He is afraid that he is no longer attractive. He notices that his body is no longer as strong as it used to be, and he is afraid that he will lose all his physical strength as he moves into old age. He is afraid that he is no longer competent at work.

Bernie's fears are only slowly emerging from his shadow. Bernie was always told that men aren't afraid of anything, so fear is deep in his shadow, and it is hard for him to face the fears that he now feels. The major manifestation of his fear is his obsession with his hair. As long as he spends his emotional energy hating his hair, he doesn't have to face the other fears. His hair has become the center of so much attention because, in effect, all his fears are connected to his hair.

Fears about what to expect in the second half of life are a very common experience at midlife. Many people of faith feel ashamed to acknowledge the fears, because obviously our faith should carry us through. Many feel that faith and fear are mutually exclusive.

Just like anger, our fears are a good source of information about what is important to us. Openly discussing our fears concerning the second half of life can help us decide what actions to take. Many midlife folks are more committed to exercise than ever before because they know that fitness will help them navigate the second half of life. That commitment to fitness came from honestly facing some of their fears about aging.

Some of the fears of aging are based on the reality of the physical decline that will continue to happen in the second half of life. One of the tasks of midlife is to embrace a dialectic that affirms both the reality of this decline but also acknowledges the potential for many new and wonderful things as we age.

When we face our fears, we will begin to be able to look to our faith to transform the meaning of these real or potential losses. We will be able to pursue the hope that our faith holds out to us.

Good Things and Unfulfilled Potentials

My mother is an extremely tidy person. We joke that she puts the dishes in the dishwasher before we have finished eating. I have struggled with tidiness all my life. I like tidy and clean spaces. I just don't like creating them.

I have a view of myself as an extremely messy and chaotic child. Recently I dug out my Barbie dolls because I wanted to sell them. Two of my Barbies were still in their boxes, and I had a tangle of clothes, shoes, jewelry, and purses in another box. I went to a doll dealer, and she and I sorted through all the clothes and other items, comparing the outfits to the original catalogs, which the dealer owned. To my surprise, every Barbie clothing outfit I owned could be matched with the accessories that had originally come with it. I had not lost one item, not one of those tiny shoes, earrings, or purses.

That day with the doll dealer helped me realize that I was actually a moderately tidy child, but in the face of my mother's unbelievable level of tidiness, I felt that I could never measure up. So I gave up trying, and I shoved tidiness into my shadow. By the time I was a teenager, I was getting messier, and in my 20s and 30s, I was very untidy indeed.

At midlife, I am rediscovering tidiness. It is emerging from my shadow. It's a hard struggle to let it emerge, because I have spent so many years nurturing habits of untidiness. But I'm making progress. I actually hang up my clothes, or put them away, almost all the time now, right when I take them off. My husband has been advocating that habit since we got married 23 years ago, and it has finally dawned on me that when you drape your clothes over a chair or drop them on the floor, they get wrinkled.

Part of how I know that tidiness is in my shadow is that I am attracted to tidy people, both male and female. I've never had a close female friend who is untidy, and I find that the men I am attracted to all happen to be tidy. I have come to believe that the drive to tidiness is a significant part of who I am, but that I have never chosen to nurture that part of me because I was always so sure that I would fail.

This may seem like a rather silly or small issue to discuss. Tidiness or untidiness: who cares? Unfortunately, I've spent a lot of my life caring: feeling guilty for being untidy, wishing I could be more tidy, admiring tidy people. The emotional power of this issue for me indicates something about it is connected to my shadow.

In addition, I mention this issue of tidiness because it illustrates so clearly the way we can split off good parts of ourselves. Many women were never encouraged to manifest their true intelligence or competence, and at midlife they may experience great joy in discovering that they were intelligent and competent all along. They may also discover real obstacles in their families of origin or their current families as they begin to express their intelligence and competence.

Julia Cameron's book *The Artist's Way* helps people discover the creativity that is latent deep inside. Exploring art, music, writing, and dance has been very healing and enriching for people of all ages. At midlife particularly, exploring and developing our creative side can help us discover parts of ourselves that have been hidden for years.

Some men may find themselves crying for the first time at midlife. Some women, too! "Men don't cry," they were told. "Big girls don't cry," they heard. Tears are a wonderfully healing expression of sadness and grief. Having the freedom to cry is part of being a whole person. If the honest expression of vulnerability was not encouraged in our families of origin, however, we may have shoved down into our shadow the ability to feel pain and to cry. At midlife these undeveloped potentials may emerge.

Some people, both men and women, may not have been encouraged to express their gentler sides. Perhaps their parents were very ambitious for them, and they were encouraged always to think about how to get ahead. At midlife they discover the joys of caring for others, of coming alongside people in pain, even though it doesn't advance their careers one bit.

One of the joys in working with people at midlife is watching the emergence of all these healthy elements of their beings. Congregational leaders can expect to see the emergence of all kinds of good things at midlife: compassion for the poor or needy, increased sensitivity to others' pain, and all sorts of kindness and gentleness that are rooted in true caring rather than in the desire for superficial niceness.

Sexuality

In a first-person, anonymous story in a Seattle alternative paper, a woman describes her attraction to her son-in-law. She thinks about him all the time and has decided she is in love with him. She dreams about him, she sleeps with his T-shirt, and she longs to know that he is attracted to her, too. Yet she loves her daughter and would never do anything to hurt her, so she knows this fantasy attraction cannot possibly have a happy ending.

I would have written off this anonymous woman as an isolated, unbalanced person if I didn't know Elaine. Now in her early 40s, Elaine has experienced many changes in recent years. She had children very early and stayed home with them in her 20s and early 30s. In her late 30s, she went back to get her college degree and began working as an accountant right before her fortieth birthday.

Elaine will tell you she is happily married. She and her husband are experiencing the empty nest, and they are having a lot of fun together exploring new forms of recreation. Elaine is a consistent church attender, and her faith is important to her.

Elaine is also extremely attracted to one of her coworkers. The attraction has lasted for more than two years, and she wonders if it will ever go away. Elaine dreams about him, she thinks about him all the time, and she enjoys learning about his little habits and his likes and dislikes. She imagines making love with him. She both dreads and anticipates working with him on projects, because she knows that being with him will make the obsession worse for the next few days. She loves her husband and would never do anything to hurt him, so she knows there can be no positive outcome of this attraction.

Shadow forces are at work in Elaine's attraction. Her coworker has some personality traits that resemble Elaine's father, who abandoned Elaine's mother and Elaine at an early age and was always vilified by Elaine's mother. In addition, the coworker manifests some of the traits—particularly a laughing ability to be flexible and easygoing—that Elaine herself has always wanted but feels she lacks.

Elaine's mother was always negative about sex. Elaine enjoys sex with her husband but always wonders if there's something that she's missing in the arena of sexuality.

Elaine is dealing with all these issues in therapy. It is certainly not the role of congregational leaders to attempt to provide therapy for congregation members with issues as complex as this one, but it is important for us to realize that the members of our congregations may be dealing with deep and confusing issues about sexuality. We can help by providing classes and small groups where people can begin to talk openly about the real issues of their lives, and we can help by being generally supportive and encouraging of individuals.

For many people, all sorts of issues concerning sexuality emerge at midlife. For the person who was sexually abused in childhood and has managed to ignore it for years, midlife is often the time that the memories come back to the surface and demand to be dealt with. For people raised in sexually repressive environments, midlife often finds them facing all sorts of thoughts, feelings, and fantasies about sex that they never imagined having to deal with.

As we preach, teach, lead, and organize educational opportunities in our congregations, we are ministering to people with deep thoughts and feelings about sexuality. Because sexuality and sexual attraction are such powerful forces in people's everyday lives, we cannot afford to pretend that sex doesn't exist. Yet that is the attitude in many congregations.

A seminar on sex and our culture, a class for parents on how to talk with kids about sex, or a marriage enrichment event focused on sex in marriage can communicate to our congregations that faith and sex have some connection and that we are not in the business of trying to help people live as nonsexual beings. As we strive to help people navigate their midlife years, honesty about sexuality will help people realize that faith and sexuality are not completely separate topics.

Observing the Emergence of the Shadow

How can we know when material from our shadow is making an appearance? I have already mentioned, when I discussed my issues with regard to tidiness, that I have always been attracted to people who are tidy. Noticing how we react to people can help us observe the emergence of the shadow.

Observing How We React to People

We can begin by making a list of all the qualities we do not like in other people. This list might be very long. Then we can extract from the list the characteristics we not only dislike but hate, loathe, despise. This shorter list will tell us part of what is in our shadow. We will probably not like this list one little bit.

Certainly there are characteristics we dislike in others which are not a part of our shadow, but any time we respond to another person with excessive emotion, we need to consider that something in that person is "hooking" us. We need to ask if perhaps that particular negative characteristic might be a part of our life that we have succeeded in ignoring up until now.

The positive traits we admire in others may also indicate parts of ourselves that we have pushed out of our conscious minds for whatever reason. We can list all the qualities we deeply admire in other people. When we find ourselves saying, "I'm not like that at all," we would do well to consider whether that trait is a part of the undeveloped potential in our shadow.

Asking for Feedback from Others

When we look at other people, we can often see aspects of their personality to which they are completely blind. That means that when people look at us, they may be able to see parts of us of which we are completely ignorant.

To discover the material in our shadow, we can ask people close to us to tell us about the parts of our personality that they believe we don't see. Unfortunately, we are usually disinclined to believe what we are told. We often find ourselves thinking or saying, "What are you talking about? The last thing in the world I want to be is arrogant!" The intensity of our emotion as we deny the presence of that particular attribute is a clue that something from our shadow may be revealed.

Observing Humor

The things that we laugh at can help us see issues that are emerging from the shadow. Slapstick comedy, with all its implicit cruelty, can help us understand the repressed sadism that we hold inside us as we laugh at the misfortunes of the cartoon character. As we laugh at jokes about someone's malicious gossip, we can acknowledge our own shadow element of enjoying gossiping. Jokes about sex can help us understand the aspects of our sexuality that we have repressed.

Examining our "Slips"

Slips of the tongue can be highly revealing. When we find ourselves saying, "That was the absolutely last thing I wanted to say," or "I'm sure you know I was joking when I said that," we have a clue that possibly the shadow was making an appearance. Once, at a lunch at work, a former employee dropped by. As I said hello to him, I found myself saying in a joking tone, "We don't allow former coworkers to visit." The words came out before I knew what was happening. I couldn't believe what I had said, and I told him I was joking.

Later in the day I began to realize that I really hadn't been joking. I began to see how much I resented his presence in the workplace because it made me feel superfluous and incompetent. Issues of competence are a significant part of my shadow material.

When we are perceived in a way totally different way from what we intended, we are experiencing a "slip" of behavior. These slips can also give us valuable information to journey inward to discover more about ourselves.

When we are trying to be calm and cool, and we come across as angry and passionate and someone tells us about it, we can choose to ignore the feedback or we can examine what is inside us. When we are trying to praise someone and our spouse tells us we sounded sarcastic and paternalistic, we can listen and take our spouse's words seriously, or we can laugh it off.

Studying Our Dreams, Daydreams, and Fantasies

We may want to deny that we daydream very often or that we indulge in fantasies. William Miller, author of two books on the shadow, poses these questions: "What do we think about when there is nothing to think about? Where does our mind go: what images and fantasies invade our thoughts?"[4] He writes that daydreams and fantasies can be so contrary to the person we believe ourselves to be that they may even frighten us, and we generally do not enjoy admitting to ourselves or to others what we find in our daydreams and fantasies.

Yet we have an opportunity to learn more about ourselves. Miller writes, "In our fantasies and daydreams we discover thoughts, plans, schemes, and dreams that we are unable to accept on a conscious level. These are often fantasies of violence, power, wealth, and sexual acting out." We probably don't like to admit the existence of these aspects of ourselves. But, Miller continues, "There are also fantasies of gold and daydreams of enrichment, wherein we see ourselves as achievers of the impossible. Once again, the shadow stands ready to share its gold if we will be encounter it and reflect on it.[5] Our dreams, Miller says, can also help us access our shadow. He writes that when the shadow appears in our dreams, it often appears as a figure of the same sex as ourselves. In the dream we may find ourselves reacting to the figure in fear, dislike, or disgust. We may want to escape from this person. The tendency in dreams is to want to avoid the shadow, just as we usually want to do in conscious life.

Why Bother with the Shadow?

Maybe our tendency to avoid the material in the shadow reflects some kind of important truth. Maybe we really should just ignore all these negative aspects of ourselves and get on with trying to be loving, productive people. Maybe our congregations would be better off if we didn't pay attention to all these complex and confusing thoughts.

These are the kinds of ideas that often arise when we are discussing issues having to do with the shadow. These are the voices that come from the parts of our conscious minds that want to keep things nice, tidy, and comfortable.

Certainly it would not be appropriate to turn our congregations into places where we dwell on complex psychological issues to the exclusion of everything else. And certainly we don't want to be communities that are obsessed with sex or inner darkness. However, I do want to affirm the importance of addressing the issues presented by the shadow.

People outside faith communities often criticize hypocrisy and self-righteousness when they see it in people of faith. Some degree of honesty about our potential for evil seems to be essential in presenting to the outside world a compassionate message about the significance of faith. In addition, when we ignore our potential for evil, we negate a powerful motivation for compassionate caring for human need. Much compassion is rooted in facing our own evil. Facing that potential for darkness will enable us to love more effectively.

So many untapped potentials reside in the shadow. The drive to be nice above all else has led many congregations to embrace a view that ignores the power of human emotions such as anger and fear. Honest acknowledgment of the power of anger and fear to give us information will help our congregation members to move ahead with energy and vision. Some of this energy and vision will motivate them towards service in their congregations.

Our congregation members who are at midlife will be dealing with shadow material, whether we like it or not. We can choose to be a community that facilitates some of this personal growth. In that case, congregation members are likely to experience God as present in this confusing area of life. If we as a community decide to completely ignore these significant issues, our congregation members are more likely to experience less connection between their relationship with God and the confusing thoughts and feelings that they experience at midlife.

One of the strongest reasons to deal with the shadow is that so many church conflict situations catch us completely unaware. "I thought people of faith didn't talk in a mean way like that," we think. "In fact, I thought people of faith wouldn't even have such powerfully negative thoughts. Is something wrong with us that we are wrapped up in such a devastating conflict?"

One therapist suggests that the shadow is most visible in very painful congregational conflict situations, such as conflicts involving the termination of clergy. If negative thoughts have been completely denied in an attempt to be nice all the time, if anger and fear have been viewed as always sinful, then when negative thoughts and emotions try to emerge from the shadow, they will probably be shoved back down. Unfortunately, if we don't carefully acknowledge the reality of these powerful emotions and thoughts, they will probably come bursting out at the most embarrassing and inconvenient times, such as in the middle of a congregational meeting. All too often, as these repressed emotions and thoughts burst out of us, we find ourselves saying hurtful and negative things that we later deeply regret.

Preemptive attention to the shadow can help us avoid some of the negative interactions we dread so much. It can also help us discover previously untapped riches that will help us grow in many ways.

Questions for Reflection

Questions for you to use personally in reflection, journaling, or discussion:

1. In what ways do you consider anger and fear to be wrong or inappropriate in themselves? What do your fears and your anger teach you about your values and priorities?

2. What parts of your sexuality were discouraged when you were young? If you are seeing aspects of sexuality emerge at midlife, what new connections do you see between your sexuality and your spirituality?

In what ways does your sexuality connect you to God? What role does your faith play as you consider your sexuality?

3. If you are experiencing a new awareness of the potential for evil inside you, spend some time considering the ways compassion may also be emerging.

4. What unfulfilled potentials can you see emerging from your shadow? What small steps could you take to develop one of those potentials?

5. Consider further exploration of the material that is emerging from your shadow by

   • listing positive and negative traits you observe in others
   • asking for feedback from friends about the traits you are unaware of
   • watching your reactions to humor
   • watching your slips of the tongue and behavior
   • studying your dreams, daydreams, and fantasies.

Questions for congregational leaders:

1. In what ways could you encourage opportunities in your congregation for people to be honest about what they are really experiencing and about the darkness they may be discovering inside themselves? In what ways could you encourage your small groups to move towards a greater level of honesty and vulnerability, so that people can talk about what is really going on in their lives, about their fears, and about their anger? In what ways could you more effectively promote Twelve Step groups, either in your congregation or in the community?

2. If you are a person who preaches, in what ways could you make your sermons seem "real," in the sense that they address real issues of everyday life? If you use a printed prayer of confession in your worship, in what ways does the prayer sometimes contain honest expressions about the darkness inside each of us?

3. In what arenas could you discuss sexuality in your congregation? Possibilities include a seminar on sex and our culture, a class for parents on how to talk with kids about sex, a marriage enrichment event focused on sex and marriage.

CHAPTER 6

Who Am I?
Personality Type at Midlife

For it was you who formed my inward parts; you knit me to-
gether in my mother's womb. I praise you, for I am fearfully
and wonderfully made.

Psalm 139:13

One of the central questions of midlife is "Who am I?" This query leads to further questions of meaning and purpose in life, but those secondary questions cannot be answered without first addressing the foundational question of identity.

Understanding personality type can provide some answers to this basic question. Many people at midlife find in personality type a vocabulary that helps them describe their differences from the people around them and the unique contributions they are able to make.

In addition, personality type can help us understand some of the patterns of development in our lives that become so evident at midlife. In this chapter we will explore the basics of personality type and the patterns of type development that are significant at midlife. In the next chapter we will explore patterns of spirituality based on type.

What Is Personality Type?

In 1923 a remarkable book, *Psychological Types* by Carl Jung, was translated into English for the first time. A mother-daughter pair read the book with great enthusiasm. They began to analyze their family members and friends along the lines of Jung's psychological type categories.

During World War II the daughter, Isabel Briggs Myers, was dismayed at the kinds of war work people she knew were choosing. She was convinced that if people understood themselves better, they would make better choices. She began to write a series of questions that would help people determine their psychological type.

Myers studied psychometrics, the statistical underpinnings that enable psychologists to evaluate the reliability of a test or instrument. She tested each of her questions to determine their statistical validity. She assembled the questions. The Myers-Briggs Type Indicator (MBTI) was born.

The MBTI is the most widely used psychological instrument today. Hundreds of thousands of people take it each year. Type is taught in work seminars and in marriage and family counseling. The principles of Jung's theory of psychological type are accessible to many because of Isabel Briggs Myers' work.

Other instruments to measure psychological type have sprung up. One of them, the Keirsey-Bates Temperament Sorter, is available on the Internet. Although it may be less accurate than the MBTI because it was not subjected to the same kind of validity testing, more than 250,000 people take it each year online. Two other instruments have been subjected to validity testing. One of them, the Murphy-Meisgeier Type Indicator for Children, measures type in children and young teens. Another instrument, the Personality Profiler, was written in the 1990s, so the language and questions are very up-to-date.

The Basics of Personality Type

Personality type, or psychological type, is based on a series of dichotomies that Jung observed as he counseled many people. He noticed that everyone is sometimes energized by the outer world of people, things, and activities and other times energized by the inner world of thoughts, feelings, and reflections. He gave the name "extraversion" to the pattern of being energized by the outer world and "introversion" to the pattern of being energized by the inner world. He noticed that most people seem to find their energy more consistently in one or the other; some people are more comfortable with extraversion and some people are more comfortable with introversion.

Jung also noted two functions of the brain: taking in information and making decisions about information. He observed two different styles of taking in information: sensing, which focuses on the facts, and intuition, which focuses on the meaning of the facts. He also observed two different styles of making decisions about information: thinking, which uses a process of analytical logic, and feeling, which considers human values and harmony in deciding. All of us use sensing, intuition, thinking, and feeling, but Jung noticed that people seem to be more comfortable with one way of taking in information and one way of making decisions.

Isabel Briggs Myers used Jung's vocabulary as she devised the MBTI, so the first three letters of a person's psychological type reflect Jung's observations. Myers, in her countless interviews with family members and friends regarding type, noticed that people seem to have one additional preference: some seemed more comfortable taking in information and some preferred to move to the decision-making stage more rapidly. The fourth letter of a person's psychological type reflects this preference in the outer world. Perceiving refers to the preference for continuing to take in information as we live our lives in the outer world. Judging refers to the preference for moving quickly to the decision-making phase.

Unfortunately, some of the vocabulary having to do with psychological type is easy to misinterpret. When talking about type, we use "introversion" and "extraversion" to refer to the source or direction of energy. In our society, "introversion" is often interpreted as shyness, and "extraversion" is often used to describe loud, peppy behavior. When people explore personality type, they may find that introverts are somewhat more likely to be shy than extraverts, or that extraverts are slightly more likely to manifest their energy in a loud, peppy way. However, the issues concerning extraversion and introversion go much deeper than such superficial behavior. In addition, I certainly know many bold and intrepid introverts and many quiet extraverts who are very good listeners.

In the world of psychological type, we use the word "intuition" to describe a process of taking in information that asks questions of meaning, purpose, and long-range implications. "Intuition" here does not refer to a dictionary definition such as "comprehension without effort of reasoning; instinctive knowledge." People of any type can seem to have instinctive knowledge.

The decision-making style called "feeling" does not have any connection to what we call feelings or emotions. People of any type can be passionate, emotive, and highly in touch with their feelings. We use "feeling" in psychological type to describe a way of making decisions based on people-centered values and the desire for harmony, in contrast to the thinking style of deciding, which is fueled by a concern for truth and logic.

We use "judging" to express a preference for making decisions over remaining in the state of taking in information. This word has nothing to do with being judgmental. People of any type can leap to negative conclusions about people.

Extraversion and Introversion (E and I)

Extraversion and introversion address the issue of where we find and direct our energy. All of us, on some occasions, are energized by people, things, and events in the external world around us. All of us, from time to time, find ourselves focusing our energy on this outer world of people, things, and activities. When we get energy from things and people outside of ourselves, or when we focus our energy on things and people outside of ourselves, we are extraverting or using extraversion.

All of us, on some occasions, find ourselves focusing our energy on what is going on inside of us: memories, reflections, ideas, plans, images, hopes, and dreams. All of us, from time to time, derive energy from this inner world. When our inner activities are the focus of our energy or the source of our energy, we are introverting or using introversion.

Most of us feel more comfortable either introverting or extraverting. We call people introverts or extraverts depending on which world they are more comfortable in, the outer world or the inner world. It is extremely important to remember that all of us use both introversion and extraversion. Describing oneself as an introvert does not mean that we cannot function in the outer world. It means that we might need to exert slightly more energy to do so because it doesn't come as naturally. Extraverts definitely can access the inner world of ideas and reflections. It may require more energy for them to do so than they need if they are focused on the outer world, but they are not necessarily totally out of touch with what they are thinking and feeling.

Most of us can identify whether the inner world or the outer world gives us more energy and joy when we focus on it. If we aren't aware whether our energy more often comes from and goes toward the inner or outer worlds, usually our friends and families can give us helpful information about what they observe in us.

Introversion and extraversion have profound implications for spirituality, particularly for spirituality at midlife. In almost every faith tradition, there are activities that fit an extraverted picture: active service of the poor, visiting the sick, worshipping in a group, decorating a worship space, finding God in creation, discussing an issue from the Bible, or discussing in a group the future of the community. Equally present in most faith traditions are activities that we could consider introverted: praying or meditating alone, reading the Bible or other important books, attending silent retreats, cultivating personal memories of past religious experiences, writing thoughts and feelings in a journal, and exploring deeply held values that come from faith.

Most people, whether they are introverts or extraverts, will have a variety of expressions of faith that come from both patterns. Before midlife, most introverts say that their preferred expressions of faith are introverted, and most extraverts say that their favorite and comfortable expressions of faith are extraverted. Before midlife, people need to be challenged to accept the different expressions of faith as equally healthy and equally important. Congregation members need help from their leaders to accept each other and the variety of expressions of religious conviction.

At midlife, things get more complicated. Two forces are at work at midlife that have profound implications in this area.

First, at midlife most people find joy and satisfaction in developing weaker areas. This is true in countless areas of life, and this is a significant factor in every one of the areas of psychological type. At midlife, many introverts find themselves drawn toward expressions of faith that connect them with the created world and with people and activities. At midlife, many extraverts begin to find joy in exploring more inward and solitary expressions of faith.

The second force at work at midlife is a tendency to turn inward. Because midlife is often a time of evaluating our purpose and direction in life, reflection plays a large part in the midlife journey. Most people at midlife turn inward to some extent, finding more satisfaction in journaling, meditation, prayer, and other quiet, reflective activities.

When we overlay this drive towards reflection and quietness with the tendency for most people to develop weaker areas, we find that extraverts particularly can experience a huge change in their spirituality at midlife.

One extraverted woman, Jana, experiences great joy in a Sabbath pattern she adopted in her early 40s. She works in sales and loves people, the more the better! She used to fill her Sundays with church, meals with family and friends, or outings. She recently adopted Saturday as her Sabbath. She spends her Saturdays completely alone, thinking, praying, reading the Bible, and reflecting on memories of God in her life.

Jana began to wonder whether she really might be an introvert. In fact, after a year of this new Sabbath pattern, she became convinced she's an introvert. Her friends, however, assured her that they continued to see her pattern of great energy in settings with lots of people. This pattern fits with extraversion. Her newly discovered love of solitude—one day a week—fits with what we know about midlife spirituality for extraverts.

Introverts at midlife don't seem to change as dramatically. Some introverts at midlife report increased connection with God through extraverted forms of spirituality. At the same time, many introverts are drawn inward to ponder the midlife questions of meaning and purpose, which continues their natural focus on quiet spirituality.

It might seem that introverts would feel tension at midlife from being pulled towards their opposite—extraversion—while they are experiencing the midlife inward turn. As I have talked with introverts at midlife, I haven't heard them express that tension. I have heard plenty of comments like, "I'm experiencing such joy in connecting with the creation. I could never do it before in this way." That suggests an increased comfort in the outer world. I've also heard many comments like, "Finally, at last, at midlife the people my own age are acknowledging the importance of the inner life of faith. It is such a relief to have some support." Other introverts say things like, "I never let myself develop my private, inner life the way I wanted to, because I was trying to achieve. Now I'm giving myself that freedom." I hear a lot of relief and freedom expressed by introverts at midlife.

Recent studies show that introverts and extraverts each make up about half of the population in the United States. Earlier studies had indicated that extraverts outnumber introverts, which seemed logical because our culture appears to be so extraverted. Now we have to develop a different explanation for the emphasis on extraversion in our culture. I suspect our frontier mentality and historic love of adventure have contributed to the powerful emphasis on activity and achievement that we sense in our culture, an emphasis which makes us label our culture as extraverted.

Whatever the source of this extraverted emphasis in American life, many introverts spend their 20s and 30s trying to fit in. This exhausting effort to develop relational and negotiation skills, to work hard and succeed, and to keep up the social patterns expected of young adults can leave introverts pretty worn out as they approach midlife. The turn inward that naturally happens for many at midlife can be welcome indeed for many introverts.

Sensing and Intuition (S and N)

Our brains perform two major functions. We take in information and we make decisions about information. Psychological type describes two ways of taking in information and two ways of making decisions about information. The two ways of taking in information are sensing and intuition.

When we are using sensing, we begin and remain with the information absorbed by the five senses. Sensing is oriented to the present reality of what we can hear, smell, see, taste, and touch. We also use sensing to connect us to memories of past experiences. Sensing helps us access the information received earlier through the five senses. When we use sensing, we work sequentially, noticing things in the order in which they present themselves to us. Sensing enables us to observe the specifics of one particular tree in a large forest.

When we are using intuition, we begin with the five senses. We receive enough sensory information to make a leap to the bigger questions of meaning and purpose. Intuition is interested in patterns: How do these trees fit together to make a forest? What is the purpose of the forest? How is the purpose connected to the pattern of the trees? When we use intuition, we do not work sequentially; instead we move around so we can continue to see the big picture. Intuition relies on symbols and metaphors to make sense of life. Intuition connects us to the future possibilities in a situation.

All of us use sensing and intuition. Most of us feel comfortable using one more than the other. People who prefer sensing tend to be matter-of-fact, practical people, who are observant about life's details and who enjoy present reality and past memories. People who prefer intuition tend to be more abstract in their thinking and talking. They tend to enjoy discussing big-picture planning for the future and questions of meaning.

The patterns of sensing and intuition have significant implications for understanding spirituality and expressions of faith. Sensing connects us to God as creator because it is sensing that enables us to taste, smell, see, feel, and touch the beauty of the physical world we inhabit. Intuition connects us to the God of mystery who is made known through metaphor and image: God as light, God as the rock, God as shepherd.

The great festivals and celebrations of many religions draw on both sensing and intuition for their power. The Passover meal includes dipping herbs in salt water to remind us of the tears and suffering of the people of Israel in Egypt. Coupling the taste of the salt water with the memory of a past event is a powerful sensing combination. The haroseth—a mixture of raisins, grated apples, and honey—reminds us by its texture of the mortar used by the people of Israel to make bricks in Egypt. The other Passover foods, repeated year after year, reinforce this sensing experience.

The Passover also includes a strong intuitive component. What does it mean that God delivered the children of Israel from the power of the Pharaoh of Egypt? It means that God is the deliverer. What is the Passover about? It reminds us that God doesn't forget his people, that God continues to work in history, and that we can count on God in the future.

Hanukkah also has both sensing and intuitive components. The traditional foods and the dreidel game make the present and past real. The holiday centers around an historical event involving light in the temple, and this emphasis on light as a metaphor engages the intuitive part of our minds.

The Christian sacraments of baptism and communion also have sensing and intuitive components. Baptism involves the tactile experience of water (sensing) as a symbol for new birth (intuition). The communion elements of bread and wine keep us in touch with sensory experience. The meaning of the communion engages our intuition.

Before midlife most of us develop a spirituality based on either sensing or intuition, but not both. The true genius of so many religious celebrations and sacraments is that they enable people with both preferences to engage in the religious experience. At midlife most people begin to develop competence for their less preferred areas, so it is natural at midlife for a sensing type to develop an interest in the great metaphors of faith. It is also natural at midlife for intuitives to experience God more and more through activities such as hiking or creating something with their hands. Religious celebrations and sacraments become infused with great meaning after midlife because we are able to experience so much more of what they bring to us because we are more competent with both sensing and intuition.

About three-quarters of the U.S. population has a preference for sensing, while approximately one-quarter prefer intuition. Everyone tends to ask questions of meaning and purpose at midlife, whatever their type, but for the sensing type these questions will feel more unfamiliar and uncomfortable. Intuitives have probably been asking a certain number of questions about meaning and purpose all their lives, but these questions will probably feel particularly new and troubling for those with a sensing preference, which includes the majority of people in most congregations.

Thinking and Feeling (T and F)

We have discussed two ways of taking in information—sensing and intuition. Now we will turn to two ways of making decisions about information—thinking and feeling.

When we are using thinking, we are weighing information using criteria of analytical logic and objective truth. When we use thinking, we can usually articulate the reasons for the judgment we are making. Thinking motivates us to ask questions, to confront what we believe to be untrue, and to strive for consistency and coherence.

Feeling is a process of making decisions that looks at the implications of the decision on people. Remember that the word "feeling," when discussing type, does not mean feelings or emotions. In psychological type, feeling is concerned for harmony among people and harmony with important values. Feeling motivates us to look at people's needs, concerns, and passions as we weigh the pros and cons of a decision. Feeling motivates us to affirm process and collegiality. Often when we make a decision based on feeling, it is difficult to articulate a set of reasons for the decision. We simply know it is best for the people involved.

Each of us uses both thinking and feeling. Most of us will feel more comfortable using one or the other of them. People who prefer thinking are more likely to come across as straightforward, articulate, and reasoned in their approach. People who prefer feeling are more likely to come across as warm, affectionate, and caring.

Let's consider the situation of a congregation trying to decide whether or not to construct a needed addition to their building. The people who prefer thinking are more likely to want to make the decision based on whether the finances are in place, whether the necessary resources are available within the congregation for the upheaval caused by construction, and whether or not these particular construction plans make the most sense. People who prefer feeling are more likely to want to consider first the impact on the congregation. Is this the right time to build when we consider the several recent deaths in the congregation? Maybe more time will be required for mourning? Or perhaps we should move more quickly than might be financially wise because of the ministry needs that this addition would address.

We use both thinking and feeling in the spiritual life. When we use thinking in the arena of faith, we are motivated to study, ask questions, and find answers that we can live with. We focus on God as the source of truth, and we connect with God through our minds. When we use feeling in the arena of faith, we are motivated to reflect the love of God through caring for people, and we connect with God through our hearts.

The great religious traditions of the world address both thinking and feeling concerns. In Judaism we see the stress on the study of the Law, coupled with an emphasis on deeds of mercy. The same is true in Christianity. Jesus spoke uncompromising truth when he confronted behavior he considered to be violations of God's will, yet he touched a leper and talked gently with women from all walks of life.

Before midlife most of us have a preference for either thinking or feeling in our spiritual life. At midlife, as we begin to develop less preferred areas, we can find ourselves doing new things. The cognitive thinking type, for example, who has always enjoyed intense intellectual discussions about faith, might find himself enjoying others' faith stories in new ways. The simple joys of faith touch him deeply. He watches people's faces as they come back from receiving communion, and their joy and their tears move him deeply. He will never lose his ability to analyze and think clearly, but he is more rounded now as he connects with the people around him more deeply.

The feeling type, who has enjoyed 20 years of service activities, may find herself embarking on serious study of her faith. She begins to study biblical languages, attends classes, and eventually gets a graduate degree. She will never lose her warmth, but at midlife she begins to become more articulate and clear about her own faith tradition.

Thinking and feeling are the only type preferences that are linked to gender. About two-thirds of men in the United States prefer thinking and about two-thirds of women prefer feeling. This raises significant identity questions for men who prefer feeling and women who prefer thinking. These men and women may need to experience significant growth in self-acceptance at midlife as they realize more fully the implications of being different from the majority.

Several writers report a male-female flip-flop at midlife. Men often become more interested in relationships, longing for a deeper connection with their spouses, children, and friends. Women often find their stride professionally at midlife when the responsibilities for parenting have diminished. Some of this flip-flop can be attributed to the fact that two-thirds of men will be developing feeling at midlife after spending their first thirty or forty years functioning largely in the thinking realm. And the same can be said of two-thirds of women. After spending 30 or 40 years primarily using feeling, they may be developing thinking at midlife, which can manifest itself in increased drive towards mastery and competence.

Judging and Perceiving (J and P)

The fourth preference refers to the way we live our lives in the outer world. If we prefer to remain in a state of taking in information, if we tend to feel uncomfortable and penned in after making a decision, then we probably have a preference for perceiving. If we prefer to move to the decision-making stage, if we feel comfortable and at ease after decisions are made, then we probably have a preference for judging.

People who prefer perceiving usually appear flexible and easygoing. They enjoy responding to the needs of the moment. They enjoy keeping options open. They may have trouble making decisions when necessary.

People who prefer judging usually enjoy calendars and planning. They often feel uneasy in the information-gathering stage, wishing to move on to the comfort of making a decision. They enjoy having things settled, and they may sometimes make decisions too quickly just to enjoy the peaceful sensation of having made the decision.

In the U.S. population, people who prefer judging (55 percent) only slightly outnumber those who prefer perceiving (45 percent). In most congregations, people with the judging preference will outnumber people with the perceiving preference much more dramatically. Research shows that people with the combination of sensing and perceiving preferences are significantly underrepresented in the North American religious scene. One hypothesis for their absence suggests that people with both sensing and perceiving preferences are likely to find spiritual experience through recreation. Instead of attending church or synagogue, many people with preferences for both sensing and perceiving are spending their Saturdays and Sundays hiking, skiing, canoeing, river rafting, playing sports, and simply enjoying life.

One person with SP preferences who very rarely attends church said, "Life is a great gift and the way to thank the giver is to enjoy it." This statement provides some good guidance for many people at midlife in congregations. One midlife task is to find avenues of joy, to find places where we connect with the fact that life is a huge gift. For the majority of people in congregations who prefer judging, this will involve developing the uncomfortable capacity for remaining in the perceiving mode. When our options are open, when we can flex with the needs of the moment, we are more likely to be able to stay in the present and enjoy the gift of life.

It may be threatening to congregational leaders to imagine affirming the statement, "Life is a great gift and one way to thank the giver is to enjoy it." It may seem that if we say that too often, we will reduce our attendance in worship services and we will lose all our volunteers! In the midst of our desire to encourage consistent spiritual disciplines such as worship attendance and regular volunteer service, we must be careful to embrace the inborn patterns of human development, which will include for many an increased drive for flexibility and openness at midlife.

For many at midlife, lifelong patterns and practice of spiritual disciplines provide an anchor in the midst of chaotic feelings. Some people with a perceiving preference, however, may have resisted developing any kind of spiritual routine in their early adulthood. For them, the journey of midlife may involve finding consistent spiritual disciplines to follow for the first time in their lives. These disciplines may include daily prayer or meditation, Sabbath observance, regular Bible study, consistent attendance at weekly worship.

As congregational leaders, then, we need to hold a tension here. This is one of the many paradoxes of midlife. We need to help people at midlife embrace spiritual disciplines. These disciplines may have long been meaningful to them or may be new. At the same time, we need to encourage a kind of flexibility and openness to God's presence in each moment.

The Four Letters of Personality Type

When you understand your preferences in each of the four areas, you can then use four letters to describe your type. My own type is INTJ. That means I have preferences for introversion, intuition, thinking, and judging.

Remember the four functions of the brain: two ways of taking in information (sensing and intuition) and two ways of making decisions about information (thinking and feeling). Looking at my type again, we can see that I use two of those four functions most easily: intuition and thinking. That means that as I approach and enter midlife, I will probably be developing my ability to use the other two, less preferred functions—sensing and feeling.

The J at the end of my type says that I enjoy functioning in the outer world in a decision-making mode. That means I use my decision-making function—thinking—in the outer world. When we use thinking in the outer world, we call it "extraverted thinking." I also use one of my more preferred functions in the inner world. That would be intuition, and we call it "introverted intuition." Because I am an introvert, and the inner world is my more preferred arena, I use introverted intuition more than any other function. Therefore, we call introverted intuition my dominant function.

Every four-letter type has a dominant function, an auxiliary (or second) function, a third function, and a fourth function, which we call the inferior function. See table A on page 106 to see these functions delineated for each type.

Most people develop the use of their functions over their life in order of preference. In early childhood most of us develop the use of our dominant function. In our teens we tend to develop our auxiliary function. In our 20s and early 30s, we usually develop our third function. Beginning around 35, we tend to begin developing our inferior function.

This development of the third and fourth functions can cause confusion in determining our correct type. Because we are developing our third function in early adulthood and our inferior (fourth) function in our 30s and 40s, we may answer the questions on a type inventory in a way that reflects our current pattern of growth, rather than our lifelong patterns of behavior.

For example, Brigit's type preferences are INTP. You can see that Brigit's dominant function is introverted thinking by checking table A on page 106. Unlike me (INTJ), Brigit has a P at the end of her four type letters. That means she prefers to remain in a state of taking in information, or perceiving, in the outer world. Brigit's preferred perceiving function is intuition, so that's what she uses in the outer world. Since Brigit is an introvert, her more favored world is her inner world, and she uses thinking in that arena. Therefore, her dominant function is introverted thinking.

Because of Brigit's preference for introverted thinking, she has spent most of her life as a very inquisitive person who loves to explore new ideas. Around age 40, Brigit found herself thinking deeply about her values. She found herself deeply concerned about harmony among the people around her. Brigit's inferior function is feeling, so it makes sense that at midlife she would find herself exploring what is important to her. Her feeling function was beginning to develop. This concern for harmony and values was so significant in her thoughts and seemed to be such a strong preference and preoccupation, that Brigit spent a couple of years in her early 40s convinced that her true type was INFP.

Now Brigit has integrated that passion for figuring out her values, and she is engaged again in the relentless intellectual exploration that is typical for an INTP. She is more rounded now, because she knows better how to

Table A

CHART OF FUNCTIONS

	Dominant #1	Auxiliary #2	Tertiary #3	Inferior #4
ISTJ	S (I)	T (E)	F	N (E)
ISFJ	S (I)	F (E)	T	N (E)
INFJ	N (I)	F (E)	T	S (E)
INTJ	N (I)	T (E)	F	S (E)
ISTP	T (I)	S (E)	N	F (E)
ISFP	F (I)	S (E)	N	T (E)
INFP	F (I)	N (E)	S	T (E)
INTP	T (I)	N (E)	S	F (E)
ESTP	S (E)	T (I)	F	N (I)
ESFP	S (E)	F (I)	T	N (I)
ENFP	N (E)	F (I)	T	S (I)
ENTP	N (E)	T (I)	F	S (I)
ESTJ	T (E)	S (I)	N	F (I)
ESFJ	F (E)	S (I)	N	T (I)
ENFJ	F (E)	N (I)	S	T (I)
ENTJ	T (E)	N (I)	S	F (I)

S (I) means sensing used in the introverted world. We call this introverted sensing. In the same way T (E) means thinking used in the extraverted world. We call this extraverted thinking.

Most people develop competence in using their dominant function in childhood, their auxiliary function in their teen years, their tertiary function somewhere around ages 20 to 35, and their inferior function between 35 and 50.

The dominant function is used in the preferred attitude (extraversion or introversion). The auxiliary and inferior (the second and fourth) functions are used in the opposite attitude from the dominant function. There is disagreement about the attitude of the third, or tertiary, function. It is left blank on this chart because it seems to vary with the individual.

access her values and she knows more of how to act on her concern for harmony among people.

As we enter midlife, most of us are growing in competence in using our inferior function. As we move to the later stages of midlife, most of us will experience a kind of integration like Brigit did. We will have become more competent in using our dominant function, because it will be better informed by all the other functions.

How Is Type Helpful?

Many of us grew up in families that affirmed that there was one right way of doing everything. For those of us who grew up in the 1950s and early 1960s, the dominant American culture affirmed a particular way of thinking and behaving. Even in the late 1960s and early 1970s, when ethnic diversity began to be affirmed, there were still a lot of cultural messages telling us to behave in a certain way, and even worse, to be a certain way.

The language of type helps us to describe the diversity of human personality. Certainly there are many other issues and schemes that help us understand human diversity, such as birth order, ethnic origin, education level, and socioeconomic level. The best aspect of personality type is that all the descriptors are neutral. There is positive language to describe both the quiet introvert and the active extravert. There is positive language to describe the planful judging type and the flexible perceiving type. This positive language can be very helpful at midlife as we are trying to complete the task of growing up: to leave behind our parents' and our culture's values and discover our true selves and our own significant priorities.

In addition, psychological type helps us describe and understand the powerful forces at work at midlife that impact our spiritual lives. Because so many are turning inward at midlife, the introvert who has struggled to succeed in a very extraverted profession may find more peace and self-acceptance. Because of the development of opposites at midlife, an extravert may discover the joys of solitude and contemplative prayer. A judging type may find surprising contentment in increased flexibility.

God made us all as unique individuals, and psychological type, in a small way, can help us affirm the joy of our unique creation and the wonder of continual growth. God works in such a variety of ways through wonderfully diverse people. It is a gift to be able to observe such complexity and richness.

Questions for Reflection

Questions for you to use personally in reflection, journaling, or discussion:

1. Do you know your preferences in each of the four type dichotomies?

    -   introversion/extraversion
    -   sensing/intuition
    -   thinking/feeling
    -   judging/perceiving

    If not, consider buying or getting from the library one of the following excellent books that present the basics of type:

    -   *Gifts Differing* by Isabel Briggs Myers
    -   *LifeTypes* by Sandra Hirsh and Jean Kummerow
    -   *Type Talk* by Otto Kroeger and Janet M. Thuesen
    -   *I'm Not Crazy, I'm Just Not You* by Roger R. Pearman and Sarah C. Albritton

2. Spend some time reflecting on or writing about your four preferences, or as many of your preferences as you think you know. Think about situations in which you have benefited from being the way you are. Consider the ways your type has impacted your faith development. Spend some time thanking God for the way you are made and the ways you have developed.

3. Spend some time thinking about or writing about issues having to do with extraversion and introversion, particularly as they affect your faith. Think about the ways you have benefited from being either an introvert or extravert. Think about the ways you are being drawn in the opposite direction at midlife, and consider ways you can encourage such development without pushing yourself too much. Spend some time thanking God for the gifts of extraversion and introversion.

Questions for congregational leaders:

1. In what ways does your congregation value some of the type prefer-
    ences over others? Are certain types of people more welcome in lead-
    ership positions than others? Are certain patterns of service that are
    related to specific types more valued than others? If so, what could you
    do to provide more balance?

2. In what ways do you as a community value extraverted expressions of
    spirituality more than or less than introverted expressions of spiritual-
    ity? Are there opportunities in your congregation for extraverted forms
    of service, including active service of the poor, visiting the sick, wor-
    shipping in a group, decorating a worship space, finding God in creation,
    discussing an issue from the Bible, or discussing in a group the future of
    the community? Are there also opportunities for introverted activities,
    such as praying or meditating alone, reading the Bible or other impor-
    tant books alone, silent retreats, cultivating personal memories of past
    religious experiences, writing thoughts and feelings in a journal, and
    exploring deeply held values that come from faith? If you habitually
    emphasize one of the two—either introverted or extraverted expres-
    sions of spirituality—consider ways you could provide more balance.

3. As a congregation, do you hold in tension the patterns of spirituality that
    are related to judging and perceiving? Do you encourage people to
    develop consistent patterns of spiritual disciplines? Do you also encour-
    age people to be present to the activity and gifts of God in the world
    right now? Consider ways you would provide more affirmation for both.

CHAPTER 7

Eight Spiritual Paths

There are varieties of activities, but it is the same God who activates all of them in everyone.

1 Corinthians 12:6

Elizabeth is an energetic, organized woman in her 60s. She distinctly remembers the period of her life when her faith became more real and she experienced a sense of deepened commitment to God and to her church.

She was in her forties. Her daughter had left for college and her son was in his last year of high school. She had stayed home with her children throughout their childhood years, driving them to music lessons and leading scout troops. Now she had much more free time on her hands.

Elizabeth signed up for some new volunteer commitments in the community. She also took up golf and skiing. She spent more time gardening. And she got more involved at church.

Each year, Elizabeth's Episcopal congregation held a quiet vigil between Good Friday and Easter. Congregation members were invited to sign up for an hour to come to the church building to pray. Elizabeth began signing up for an hour in the middle of the night. With each passing year, the vigil became more meaningful for her.

The minister left booklets and other reading material in the sanctuary for the participants. For the first time in her life, Elizabeth found herself reading the literature of contemplative Christianity, full of rich metaphors and images. Those hours she spent in the church in the middle of the night enabled her to crystallize some of the deeply held values that she had neglected to express for the first 40 years of her life.

She had attended church almost every Sunday of her life, but some-how in the busy years of young adulthood, she had never affirmed to herself or to God just how important her faith was to her. Apart from weekly church attendance, the actions of her life had not reflected a commitment to God and to spiritual growth. She realized she wanted that to change.

Like an ocean liner ponderously turning in the middle of the Atlantic, Elizabeth experienced a gradual but significant turn during her 40s. Her faith began to take center stage in her life. Her church involvements over the years that followed enabled her to consider more deeply what she really believed and to act on those beliefs.

In her early 50s, when she served on the church vestry, Elizabeth ex-plored her own priorities for congregational life. As chair of the steward-ship campaign in her late 50s, she explored her own beliefs about the con-nections between faith and financial generosity. She attended more special worship services on saints' days and came in contact over and over again with the literature of contemplative Christianity with its metaphors and im-ages of faith.

Elizabeth's story illustrates the ways our faith experience changes at midlife. When we understand the categories expressed in psychological type, we can see some interesting patterns of spirituality at midlife.

Elizabeth's personality type preferences are ESTJ: extraversion, sens-ing, thinking, and judging. She is innately friendly, straightforward, matter-of-fact, organized, tidy, firmly grounded in the present, and closely con-nected to the physical world of the senses. At midlife Elizabeth began to experience connection to the two functions, intuition and feeling, which are not her preferred functions. Her spiritual growth after midlife demonstrates this new connection.

Spirituality based on intuition, particularly introverted intuition, is the spirituality of images, metaphors, and possibilities. As Elizabeth sat in the darkened church building in the middle of the night between Good Friday and Easter, she experienced attraction to this kind of spirituality for the first time in her life. Many aspects of weekly worship began to connect her to these images. She came to appreciate the rich metaphors of light and dark-ness whenever she saw candles lit in church. The bread and the wine of communion took on new meaning.

In the second half of life, Elizabeth also experienced greater connec-tion to her faith through her feeling function. When we are using feeling, particularly introverted feeling, we access our deeply held values and beliefs.

At midlife Elizabeth began to get in touch with what she really believes, and she began to act on those beliefs in new ways.

Elizabeth continues to be a practical person. She has learned that her spirituality, first and foremost, is the spirituality of action, hospitality, and friendship. She excels at organizing charity events and running the steward-ship campaign. These deeply meaningful places of service connect her to her faith and reflect her ESTJ preferences.

Her spirituality after midlife has been rounded out by faith develop-ment in her less preferred areas: introverted intuition and introverted feel-ing. These two less visible patterns of spirituality have spurred her on to new growth by connecting her to metaphors, meaning, and values. She has continued her many forms of practical, helpful, and organized service, but she now has new richness and depth that undergird her actions.

Eight Patterns of Spirituality

Each of the four functions—sensing, intuition, thinking, and feeling—can be used outwardly or inwardly, in an extraverted or an introverted manner. This makes a total of eight patterns of functioning. We can observe these eight patterns in our daily lives. Two or three of these eight ways of func-tioning will probably feel very comfortable or somewhat comfortable to us. The rest will feel uncomfortable or even completely strange to us.

When you look at table A on page 106, you can see the pattern that most people follow. Most of us are most comfortable with our dominant function, which we probably developed in early childhood. By the time we reach adulthood, most of us are also comfortable with our auxiliary func-tion. By the time we reach midlife, we will probably have developed some skills with our third (tertiary) function. Most of us still have a lot of work to do to grow in comfort in using our fourth, or inferior, function.

Some people don't follow the patterns described in table A. Whatever your type, however, you undoubtedly experience more comfort and ease using two or three of the eight functions described in this chapter. Whatever your type, one of the tasks of midlife will be to grow in competence in some of the less preferred ways of functioning. This happens on the job, in rela-tionships with family and friends, in our hobbies, and in our spirituality. The bulk of this chapter will be spent exploring these eight patterns of function-ing, with particular emphasis on what spirituality looks like in each of the eight functions.

I use the word "spirituality" to describe the patterns of reflection and action that nurture our understanding that life consists of more than the physical world around us. This book is written for Christian, Unitarian, and Jewish congregations, and each tradition would use different language to amplify what I call "spirituality." Jewish people might talk about that which connects them with the traditions and history of being the people of Israel. Unitarians might talk about reflection and action that connect them with the sacred or with the nobility of humanity. Christians might talk about patterns of prayer and action that connect them with God through Jesus Christ.

Table B

THE EIGHT FUNCTIONS

Extraverted Sensing	–	The Energizers
Introverted Sensing	–	The Stabilizers
Extraverted Intuition	–	The Crusaders
Introverted Intuition	–	The Renewers
Extraverted Thinking	–	The Organizers
Introverted Thinking	–	The Analyzers
Extraverted Feeling	–	The Encouragers
Introverted Feeling	–	The Enhancers

The names, such as "Energizers," for each of the eight functions come from Reginald Johnson's book, *Your Personality and God* (Wheaton, Ill.: Victor Books, 1988). (Originally published with the title *Celebrate My Soul.*)

Whatever the language we use, these eight patterns of spirituality are observable in each of the faith traditions. I believe these patterns of spirituality are inherent in our different personality types, created in us to link us with the part of ourselves—our soul, our spirit—that draws us to seek relationship with God. And I believe that in community we will experience all eight patterns of spirituality, as each of us has different areas of strength and weakness. We need each other for balance and richness. In community each of us is rounded out by others and together we reflect the image of God.

As we grow in an understanding of these eight patterns of spirituality, we can respond in two ways in our personal lives. First, we can observe what is already happening. At midlife we will probably notice that we are already growing into new patterns of spirituality. These new patterns will probably be connected to the functions we have used less often in the first half of life.

Second, we can use these eight patterns of spirituality as a challenge and a prescription for growth. We can consciously choose to explore new patterns of spirituality. We can try these new things because we know that midlife is a time to explore all kinds of new and different ways of living. Some of the patterns we try may not be helpful to us. Some of the patterns may prove to be deeply meaningful.

These patterns of spirituality can also be very helpful to us as congregational leaders. We can use these descriptions to evaluate and analyze our congregational programs. Do we make a way for each of these eight patterns of spirituality to be expressed in our congregational life? Is our congregational life heavily weighted towards one or two patterns of spirituality only? How can we make a way to broaden our congregational spiritual practices?

In no way do I believe that these eight patterns of spirituality describe everything about the life of the spirit. These eight spiritual paths are simply helpful tools. They are one lens to use to look at different ways that people express and experience their faith. They are one way to describe possible patterns of spiritual growth at midlife.

Extraverted Sensing: The Energizers[1]

When we are using extraverted sensing, we are connected to the present world of all that we can perceive through our senses. We are focused on the concrete present reality, and we are highly observant of objective facts.

Extraverted sensing enables the race car driver to notice the small changes in the road surface that will require him to change his pace slightly. Extraverted sensing enables the downhill skier to sense and respond to the changes in terrain. Extraverted sensing enables the interior designer to see the harmonious colors in two very different fabrics.

Extraverted sensing draws us from one strong stimulus to the next. We savor the delicious meal with all its diverse flavors, followed by the bitterness of coffee and the sweetness of chocolate. The vibrant conversation swirling around us stimulates us. When we hear the music change, we want to get up and dance.

When we are using extraverted sensing, we are in the present. Our memories from the past and our plans and dreams for the future fall away. We are connected to this here-and-now sensory reality.

The spirituality of extraverted sensing is firmly rooted in the physical world. Extraverted sensing connects us with God as creator. We experience the beauty and wonder of creation. We experience the presence of God in the handiwork of God, the immanence of God in creation.

I live in the Pacific Northwest, which has the lowest church attendance in the nation. We joke about all the people worshipping God the Creator every weekend up in the mountains. But it is really not a joke. Many people experience a spiritual connection to creation as they mountain climb, hike, kayak, sail, windsurf, or bike. People who like to camp in the mountains talk about the overwhelming number of stars at night, the crisp night air, the scent of the pine needles, the morning light reflected on a lake, and the heat of the noon sun. Many experience the presence of God in these sensations.

When we are using extraverted sensing to express our spirituality, we experience a sense of rightness in using our bodies the way they were designed. The pull of muscles can become a worshipful experience, as we know for certain that muscles were designed by God to be used strenuously just like this. Extraverted sensing spirituality can give us a sense of overwhelming joy and love as we see the beauty of a shaft of sunlight filled with dust motes, or as we feel the caressing touch of a loved one. Extraverted sensing enables us to connect with the presence of God in all that is made.

The rising interest in Celtic spirituality can be explained in part by understanding our need to connect with God the Creator. In the *Book of Kells*, a beautiful Irish medieval illuminated manuscript, a variety of little animals scamper between the lines of text. Celtic spirituality is characterized by an exuberant, enthusiastic connection with the creation as the handiwork of God.

Congregations can express extraverted sensing spirituality through eating, dancing, hugs, the Passover meal, and communion. Perhaps the most common way of expressing extraverted sensing spirituality in a congregation is through decorating the worship space. Banners and seasonal decorations give a few congregation members a chance to participate through doing the decorating, and they give everyone the opportunity to look at something beautiful during the worship service.

Attractive design of the worship bulletin, newsletter, brochure, and other congregational publications can provide another opportunity to express extraverted sensing spirituality. Other places where this kind of spirituality can be manifested are in decisions about furniture, paint, and wall decorations in church offices and other meeting rooms. The upkeep of a clean and efficient kitchen and flowers in the garden outside can also manifest a spirituality of extraverted sensing.

Introverted Sensing: The Stabilizers

When we are using introverted sensing, we take the data received through the five senses and we internalize it. We use our memories to retain this sensory data. When we are using introverted sensing, we have vivid, detailed memories of past experiences, sensations, and emotions.

When we are using introverted sensing, we are very observant of present realities. As those present realities go into our memories, we are able to connect them with past events. When we are using introverted sensing, we will be likely to notice amazingly small details such as our friend's new ring. We take present sensory data and compare it to memories of past data.

Imagine that you have a vast library in your mind. When we use introverted sensing, we arrange the books on the shelves neatly, in an order connected with the subject matter of the books. We open the books and remember the contents, then consider which other books belong alongside.

Introverted sensing spirituality involves using the memory to connect us with God. We may choose to journal about places where in the past we have experienced the reality of God. We might write about childhood memories of holidays, affection from parents, or significant events at church or synagogue. We might write about events that confused us, using the act of writing to sort through certain memories to try to make sense of them, to get them in the right place in the library of our minds.

We may use art to connect us with our past memories. We might draw the memory of a past event or a place that felt holy. We may build a model of a church or synagogue we used to attend. We might keep a rock or a feather to connect us to a specific memory.

We might use introverted sensing to draw us back to places that felt significant to us in the past. We might return again and again to a place that has particular meaning or a particular connection to a memory of God's action in our lives.

In all of these memories, introverted sensing will enable us to connect vividly with the past memory. We will be able to access very specific and graphic sensory data that is stored in our minds.

Introverted sensing also enables us to use our imagination to place ourselves in the situation described by a sacred text. The classic Christian practice of Ignatian prayer involves choosing a passage from the Bible, preferably a Gospel passage involving Jesus, and imagining ourselves as a bystander in that scene. Introverted sensing enables us to connect with the sights, smells, and sounds of the scene. We are able to picture Jesus touching the leper or raising a boy from the dead. We may then be able to imagine Jesus touching us in the same way.

Introverted sensing spirituality connects us with the creeds and traditions of our faith. Using traditional prayers for meditation may be meaningful. Upholding traditions in the congregation may seem important. We use introverted sensing when we record congregational history in a scrapbook or videotape or plan a celebration of the congregation's anniversary.

Introverted sensing spirituality enables us to be comfortable with routines and set spiritual practices. It is no accident that many Catholic monks have strong preferences for introverted sensing. To nurture introverted sensing spirituality, a visit to a monastery may be helpful, particularly if you can participate in the rhythmic patterns of worship and service that have nurtured faith for so many centuries.

Extraverted Intuition: The Crusaders

When we are using extraverted intuition, we try to perceive the widest range of possibilities inherent in a given situation. Extraverted intuition is like a sixth sense that "sees" things that are not actually there. Extraverted intuition enables us to see beneath the surface and it enables us to perceive the possibilities that can grow out of present reality.

Extraverted intuition drives us towards new opportunities and new challenges. When we are using this function, we are drawn to adventure and exciting prospects. We see the best possible outcomes. We are able to see and articulate significant visions for the future.

The spirituality of extraverted intuition is the spirituality of hope. Extraverted intuition enables us to pray with true expectation for change and to establish lofty, ambitious goals that will meet human need. Extraverted intuition enables us to see God's hand at work in human life bringing health, wholeness, healing, and redemption. We are optimistic about the future because we know God is faithfully and lovingly at work in our world.

Extraverted intuitive spirituality also enables us to feel hopeful about what people can achieve. We are filled with hope because we see such potential in human beings; we see the love, care, and faithfulness manifested by people all around us, so we know humans can rise above their difficulties. We know they can act in love, so we are able to hope for the best and dream of great human achievement in every possible area.

When we are using extraverted intuition, we can look at "impossible" situations and, rather than giving in to despair, we are able see the possibilities for positive movement. What others might view as an obstacle or insurmountable problem looks like an intriguing challenge when we are using extraverted intuition. This kind of spirituality frees us to use imaginative and innovative possibilities to find solutions.

Extraverted intuition is also the spirituality of symbolic expression in community. A church for homeless women in Seattle offers an unusual ritual at each worship service. The women are invited to write down the negative things in their lives that are holding them back. Then they file forward and burn the slips of paper in a bowl, with the pastor blessing them as they pass. This kind of external expression of the symbolic reality of God's removal of sin and sickness fits beautifully with extraverted intuitive spirituality.

When we are using extraverted intuitive spirituality, we will probably enjoy traditional image-filled rituals in worship, such as communion and the lighting of Advent wreaths. But the greatest joy will be in coming up with new expressions of symbolic meaning for the community to enjoy.

Extraverted intuitive spirituality is manifested in prayers of hopeful anticipation of God's work in the world. Extraverted intuitive spirituality also makes a significant contribution to congregational leadership. That visionary, can-do, imaginative attitude is vitally important on leadership boards, retreat planning committees, children's and youth ministry committees, and other task forces.

In a congregation where there are few lay leadership positions and all the authority for planning resides with a few individuals, people with a strong preference for extraverted intuition may feel frustrated because they find no avenue to use their abilities to generate vision and hope. Take the time to look around your congregation to make sure there are many points of access when people can discuss vision for events and programs.

Extraverted intuitive spirituality enables us to see the big picture and to generate large-scale vision. When we are using this kind of spirituality, we need to be firmly connected with others who have different gifts. We need the support of those who are able to manage details, those who can care for the people involved, and those who can ask questions about the appropriateness of implementing this particular vision.

Introverted Intuition: The Renewers

When we use introverted intuition, we are using our inner life to explore questions of meaning and purpose. In many ways, introverted intuition is the most difficult of the introverted functions to understand because in one sense it has no form. It is a tangled mess of ideas, metaphors, issues, and images. The joy of introverted intuition is exploring the possibilities that lie in the connections between all the material that is in the mind. These connections will result in insight, which is the prized goal of introverted intuition.

We talked about the image of a library in the mind. We observed that when we use introverted sensing, we arrange the books on the shelves neatly, in an order connected with the subject matter of the books. In contrast, the library of introverted intuition is a messy place with piles of unfinished books, but it is also a happy place because of all the possibilities, connections, and ideas that have been and are being explored.

The spirituality of introverted intuition fits most closely with the stereotypical patterns of contemplative or mystical prayer. Images and metaphors are a significant part of this spirituality: God as rock, shepherd, or river of life. When we are using introverted intuition, we find joy in meditating on the great themes of light and darkness, creation and chaos, grace and truth.

While most spiritualities, particularly those based in sensing and feeling, seek the good and the pure, introverted intuitive spirituality understands the need for the balance of the darkness with the light. It is here that we are able to embrace the learning experiences that come from the hard and difficult places of our lives. This is the spirituality that does not desire to gloss over the realities of human life. Instead, here we seek to find God in the very darkest parts of human life.

More than any other spirituality, this is a spirituality of silent prayer and solitary meditation. Each of the other three introverted forms of spirituality requires connections with people in order to reach full fruit. Introverted sensing spirituality needs the community to uphold traditions, introverted thinking spirituality needs other people with whom to explore questions, and introverted feeling spirituality needs the community to uphold and act on values. Introverted intuitive spirituality often appears to be content with meditation and prayer in silence, alone.

However, the outcome of effective introverted intuition is insight, and when we use this kind of spirituality, we need to be sure that we pursue avenues to share that insight. Some people with a preference for introverted intuition may have a pattern of sharing their insights too quickly and forcefully, and they may be too convinced that their insights are always right. They need to be careful not to share their insights too readily.

Others with a strong preference for this kind of spirituality will need encouragement to stay connected to community and share what they have learned through their own reflection, meditation, and prayer. Because of the utter aloneness that can feel comfortable when we are using this kind of spirituality, we have to be careful to return to community. Sharing insights may be done effectively though writing as well as talking, but both require connection to community to be effective.

This kind of spirituality can find expression in congregations in teaching positions, where quiet insight and wisdom can be expressed. Introverted intuition is also valuable in leadership positions, where the insight gained from silent exploration can be shared to provide direction for ministries and programs. This kind of spirituality can contribute wisdom, new paradigms, vision for structural change, and organizational framework for congregations.

Congregations can encourage the development of introverted intuitive spirituality by providing opportunities for silent prayer and meditation and by affirming the significance of inward, meditative spirituality. Using images and metaphors in sermons, classes, and written material can also nurture this kind of spirituality.

Extraverted Thinking: The Organizers

When we are using extraverted thinking, we are using logic and analysis to make decisions about things outside ourselves. Extraverted thinking gives us the ability to size things up in order to decide how to implement an idea. Extraverted thinking motivates us to work to improve external situations so that activities can be more effective or efficient.

Extraverted thinking spirituality carries these practical, analytical concerns into the realm of study, service, and congregational life. We can use extraverted thinking when we study a biblical text with a desire to understand and apply the text in real life. Extraverted thinking enables us to see and implement structure, so this kind of study might involve outlining themes or listing important points in a passage. This kind of spirituality will ask theoretical questions about the meaning of the text, along with practical questions about the effective application of the text in our lives.

This ability to implement structure comes into play in many other areas. Extraverted thinking enables us to exercise the kind of leadership that decisively declares what needs to be done and then also has an organized plan for implementing the decision. Lists of tasks, delegating various parts of the job, and a clear concern for the overall goal will probably all be very visible when we are using extraverted thinking in leadership.

Extraverted thinking spirituality might motivate us to volunteer to coordinate a part or all of a large fund-raising event for a favorite charity. The success of the event would be measured, in our minds, by the criteria of effective organization. Did all the volunteers know when and where to do their tasks? Did the food arrive on time and was it presented effectively? Did all the participants find their tables? Did the program run smoothly? Did all the speakers know what they were supposed to do? Did the sound system work? Did the all the parts of the event run on time?

To people who are most comfortable with intuitive or feeling spirituality, extraverted thinking spirituality can appear mechanistic and overly concerned with nonessentials such as schedule, organization, and details, rather than being focused on people and religious ideals. People with a mature, well-developed extraverted thinking spirituality really do see the creation of structure as a way to serve people and as a way to attain religious ideals. A well-run class will help people learn. A well-maintained building will be available for a variety of significant events during which people's lives may be changed. A well-designed newsletter will help congregation members access the information they need in order to be involved in the congregation.

Two characteristics of extraverted thinking spirituality can be both assets and liabilities: a tendency to be impersonal and a love of structure. The impersonal, objective nature of extraverted thinking can enable a leader to deal impartially with difficult situations, but it can also make that person seem distant and uncaring. When we are using extraverted thinking spirituality, we can fall into the trap of viewing people as things in our desire to accomplish our task and meet our goal.

The enjoyment of structure can enable the establishment of policies for congregational life that can make things happen smoothly. However, this love of structure and policies can get in the way of caring for individual needs in the congregation.

The strong goal orientation of this kind of spirituality can also result in a kind of tunnel vision that is so focused on achieving this specific goal that the big picture may be lost. When we are using the organizational gifts of extraverted thinking, we need to be very dependent on others in our community of faith. Listening to other people and validating their gifts and passions will help us avoid losing sight of the needs of people, the larger community goals, and the joy that is possible in the here-and-now, even if our goals are not achieved yet.

Congregations can nurture extraverted thinking spirituality by allowing time for questions and discussion in classes and seminars. Congregational leaders can serve those with gifts in extraverted thinking spirituality by being clear about dates and plans and by affirming that a smoothly run event honors the people involved. Be sure to look around your congregation to see if there are multiple entry points for people who like to plan events and organize activities. Be sure that you affirm the necessity of structure and policies, even while you affirm the significance of caring for individuals.

Introverted Thinking: The Analyzers

When we are using introverted thinking, we are using logic and analysis to examine things that are interior to us: our thoughts and, to some extent, our feelings. Where extraverted thinking analyzes things in the outer world for the purposes of goal setting and efficient implementation of those goals, introverted thinking usually remains in the analytical, questioning state.

Introverted thinking spirituality focuses on analysis of thoughts and ideas about faith, life, God, prayer, spiritual practice, and every possible aspect of religious life. Introverted thinking spirituality, first and foremost, is the spirituality of questions. When we use this spirituality in study, we take in the text we are studying, then we reflect on the content in an analytical way. We ask many questions, working to establish the structure and meaning of the passage. We explore the implications of the details of the passage. We are thrilled when this passage takes us to another passage. Associations of ideas and exploration of the possible significance of all the associations are the joy of introverted thinking spirituality.

The kind and quality of questions we ask when we are using introverted thinking can be very helpful in all kinds of decision making in congregations. The questions may not always be welcome, because others may want to move on rapidly to a decision, but taking the time to consider all the possible questions will lead to a better outcome.

When we are using introverted thinking spirituality, no question is off-limits. This kind of spirituality may shock the people around us by the fact that nothing is sacred, that we have to explore every possible issue. No question is unimportant.

Here's an example: Someone who is using introverted thinking comes across a reference to tarot cards in an article. This sets off a concentrated exploration of the meaning, value, history, and significance of tarot cards. Are the archetypal themes represented by tarot cards useful in some way in our spiritual journey? Do they harmonize with my current religious tradition in any way? Can people learn anything of value from tarot cards? You can imagine that in some religious settings, these questions would be utterly unwelcome and would provoke the deepest disapproval. The questioner, who was innocently pursuing an interesting chain of connected questions, might be branded as out to lunch, or worse, heretical.

Of all the eight patterns of spirituality, this one is probably the least welcome in most congregations. Questions can seem to threaten the status quo. Those of us who are more comfortable with answers rather than questions need to understand two things. First, midlife is a time of question asking. If we want to enable healthy midlife journeys, we must welcome questions. Second, there are many people for whom introverted thinking spirituality is central to their encounter with God. After all, Job and the psalms are full of questions. If we don't make a place in our congregations for questions, some people will certainly go elsewhere. And we will miss out on the richness of the kind of exploration driven by constant questioning.

We need to make certain that in our congregations there are settings where all kinds of questions are welcome. Bible study classes and groups can provide healthy environments for asking questions about the biblical text. Topical seminars can be structured to allow time for questioning in large or small groups. In sermons and other lectures, the process of asking questions can be affirmed, and acknowledgment can be made that faith does not always include answers to every question right now.

We can also nurture introverted thinking in our congregations by providing arenas to explore both thoughts and actions having to do with truth and justice, two significant values that reflect the character of God and that are intimately connected to introverted thinking.

Extraverted Feeling: The Encouragers

When we are using extraverted feeling, we are connected to the people around us, desiring to serve and care for them. Extraverted feeling drives us to embrace anything that promotes harmony between people. Extraverted feeling gives us heightened sensitivity to the realities of the social situation around us, and we are motivated to do what is necessary to smooth and ease relationships.

Extraverted feeling is oriented to the relational reality outside of us. We talk about the Jungian definition of "feeling" as values, and extraverted feeling is driven by the specific values of relational harmony and gracious connection between people.

When we are using extraverted feeling, we are more aware of the reality in the lives of the people around us than the reality of what is going on inside ourselves. When we are using extraverted feeling, for better and for worse we are unlikely to be very conscious of our own thoughts and feelings. It is wonderful to be so tuned into the needs of others, but our needs and desires will often be neglected when we are using this kind of spirituality.

Religions have long valued this form of spirituality. Being acutely aware of the human needs around us is a high value in many faith traditions. Extraverted feeling spirituality results in deeds of kindness that meet specific human needs and promote harmony. Traditional Jewish acts of mitzvah, which come from compassion, fit into this pattern of spirituality, as do the good deeds of service long valued in the Christian tradition. Fixing meals for people with new babies, driving senior citizens to doctor's appointments, volunteering at the food bank, visiting shut-ins, living in a community that provides housing for handicapped people—all of these actions can be outgrowths of extraverted feeling spirituality.

Extraverted feeling also manifests itself in prayers for people's needs. This kind of spirituality will often find expression through prayer chains or prayer meetings that receive prayer requests for all kinds of people in need. Extraverted feeling drives us to pray for jobs for the jobless, for housing for the homeless, for recovery from cancer or AIDS, and for countless other human needs.

This kind of spirituality is rooted in our understanding of God as compassionate and full of mercy. When we see human need, we cannot act any other way than mercifully.

In communities of faith there will be people who need to grow in their expression of this kind of spirituality because they have developed other areas of spirituality early in life. However, there will be others who have been using this kind of spirituality most of their adult life and will need encouragement to let someone else prepare the meals for the surgery patients who just got home from the hospital. This kind of spirituality is probably the one that is most overused in congregations, and it is the hardest to say no to, because we place such a high value on caring for people in need.

Yet people who primarily use this kind of spirituality are probably the most vulnerable to burnout. Extraverted feeling connects us to human need outside ourselves while obliterating our ability to be in touch with our own needs. This is a dangerous combination in a community that places high value on caring for people. Ministers, rabbis, and other leaders need to be very aware of the potential for burnout in this area of service.

Introverted Feeling: The Enhancers

When we are using introverted feeling, we are connected to the core values we hold inside of us. These values are invisible, and people with a strong preference for introverted feeling can appear to be very calm and dispassionate people. Yet when these deeply held values are tapped into, people with strong introverted feeling preferences can become surprisingly passionate and confrontational.

These core values can manifest themselves in a wide variety of actions. A passion for justice, for example, can manifest itself in behavior that looks almost aggressive in a situation in which someone's rights have been violated. A deeply held belief about the need to care for children can turn a quiet, reserved person into an organized activist for educational reform. A core value of caring for people can manifest itself in behavior that looks just like the behavior of extraverted feeling, but it is driven by inner conviction rather than by outer need.

The spirituality of introverted feeling, first and foremost, connects us with inner values. Because our faith traditions place importance on so many different values, there is no shortage of options to explore. Introverted feeling can drive us to care about and work towards justice for the poor, providing services for the sick and disabled, effective education for children, the prevention of child abuse, the reduction of domestic violence, or the establishment of a neighborhood community center.

In addition to connecting us to these "larger" issues, introverted feeling can motivate us to establish a regular time of day to read to our children, because we are committed to the importance of reading and the relational connection around important things. Introverted feeling might drive us to throw away our TV, adopt a stray dog, care for eagle nurslings abandoned in the wild, or drive an energy efficient car. Any of these actions can be a manifestation of introverted feeling spirituality if we see the connection between our actions and our values, and if we see those values as rooted in our faith tradition. And when we are using introverted feeling, just about every value we find inside ourselves feels like it is connected to God in some way, because introverted feeling enables us to experience God as present inside us.

Introverted feeling prayer is the prayer that connects us with faith values. Prayers for world peace, prayers for a cure for AIDS, prayers for justice for the poor, prayers for racial reconciliation—these are some of the prayers that come from introverted feeling spirituality. It is important for congregations to make a way for members to pray for some of these issues.

Congregations can nurture introverted feeling spirituality by providing arenas such as seminars and classes for exploring and discussing values and passions. This kind of spirituality can be nurtured in worship services by praying as a congregation for the great social issues of our time. It is also important that congregations provide places for activism concerning significant issues. Some congregations are connected in many ways to issues of justice, racial reconciliation, and care for the poor. Others are not. Congregational leaders need to offer affirmation for their members who are involved in making society a better place to live, even if their efforts in the community keep them from direct congregational involvement.

Combinations

Many activities that are deeply meaningful and that connect us to our spirituality have aspects of more than one of the above patterns. One example would be our relationship to our pets. For many people, caring for their pets is a very significant, though seldom mentioned, part of their spirituality.

Caring for a pet includes a large portion of extraverted sensing. Petting the fur, combing or brushing or providing other grooming, providing food, and watching the antics of the pet . . . all of these connect us to the God who created this animal. Dogs force us to get outside and experience the creation, fish amaze us with their variety of colors and shapes, and cats make us laugh when we see the odd positions they choose for sleeping. Caring for and playing with the pet often enable us to stay in the present, to forget about our sorrows from the past and our worries about the future. The amazing connection between animals and humans reminds us that we are creatures just like they are, created by the same God. All of this is a part of extraverted sensing spirituality.

This relational connection between pets and humans also comes from extraverted feeling. As we groom and care for the animal, we are striving for a harmonious relationship between the animal and ourselves, or sometimes between the pet and another pet. Our pet may connect us with other pet owners. This would be another place we might use extraverted feeling.

We may have a deeply held value that animals are important. This comes from introverted feeling. We may enjoy the organizational tasks that are part of owning a pet: planning the walks, researching the best food, keeping on top of the vaccinations. This comes from extraverted thinking.

Caring for our pet may encourage us to think about all the ways God cares for us, drawing us into the images and metaphors common to introverted intuition. Our pet may motivate us to ask questions about the role of animals in creation or the neglect of animals in our society, which moves us into introverted thinking.

Having a pet can draw us into several different patterns of spirituality at the same time. We can choose to focus on one or more of these aspects of pet ownership as we go through midlife. If we want to develop our spirituality in a certain area, we can focus on that aspect of caring for our pet.

Gardening is another hobby that draws on many parts of our being. Gardening is the most popular hobby in the United States, and it is a place where many say they experience connection with God. Gardening uses extraverted sensing as we notice all the colors, shapes, and smells of the garden. Gardening requires extraverted intuition to consider all the possibilities for plants at various seasons. Gardeners may use introverted intuition as they plan the design of their gardens. They may use extraverted feeling to consider the ways their garden could serve people by the placement of benches or the way the garden will be seen from the house or the street. Gardening may connect us with introverted feeling as we consider our values with regard to caring for creation or the importance of nurturing growing things. Gardening may require extraverted or introverted thinking to analyze the tools needed, the right timing for the seeds, or the decision of whether or not to fertilize.

A midlife person who gardens may notice new pleasures in gardening that come from using new functions in the process of gardening. Gardeners can choose to develop these different functions at midlife by concentrating on one specific aspect of gardening. A person who wants to develop extraverted sensing spirituality, for example, can choose to stay in the present sensations as they work in the garden, trying to notice and stay connected to the smells, shapes, and feel of the plants, enjoying the presence of the Creator in the creation.

The Significance of the Introverted Functions

Because of the tendency to turn inward at midlife, it is worth noting the ways in which the introverted functions enable us to address significant midlife issues. As noted in the previous chapter, both introverts and extraverts experience a pull inward at midlife. Introverts will probably find themselves developing some new extraverted functions at midlife, but they will also continue to develop introverted functions. And many extraverts will be conscious of great development of introverted functions at midlife.

Introverted sensing enables us to access important memories, along with the significant traditions and rituals that have enabled us to cope in the past. Accessing these memories and traditions can act like an anchor for us in the storms of midlife. And the memories will fuel the many questions of midlife. We can nurture introverted sensing spirituality by focusing on our memories of God's hand in our lives as we journal, pray, and meditate, and by remembering and celebrating the faith traditions that have nourished us spiritually.

Introverted intuition is concerned with meaning and connections. Midlife is a significant time to explore the meaning of our lives and the connections between the various parts of our lives. The metaphors and images common to introverted intuition can help us understand our lives in new ways. We can nurture introverted intuition spirituality by using metaphors and images as we journal, pray, and meditate, and by looking for connections between the various parts of our lives and exploring what those connections mean.

Introverted thinking, first and foremost, asks questions and follows where the questions lead. Developing introverted thinking will help us welcome all these questions dispassionately and will help us explore them in an objective, detached manner. Introverted thinking will help us rejoice when our questions lead us on to more questions. We can nurture introverted thinking spirituality by embracing questions about faith, life, God, prayer, and spiritual practice, and by taking the time to explore wherever those questions lead us.

Introverted feeling helps us access our deepest and most significant inner values. Learning to access these values and deciding how we want to act on them is a central task of midlife. We can nurture introverted feeling spirituality by exploring what we truly value and by journaling, praying, and meditating about our values and they way they come from God and connect us to God.

Understanding the role of all of these introverted functions can help us gain objectivity about the tasks of midlife. As congregational leaders, we can encourage congregational members to pursue spiritual paths that are based on each of these functions.

Many congregations have such a strongly extraverted flavor that they don't make a way for patterns of spirituality based on these introverted functions. To help members at midlife, it is extremely important that these introverted functions find expression in our congregations.

Questions for Reflection

Questions for you to use personally in reflection, journaling, or discussion:

1. Which of the eight patterns of spirituality described in this chapter are most comfortable for you? Which patterns have you used in the first half of life? Which ones give you the most comfort? Spend some time reflecting back over the years and being thankful for the ways you have grown and benefited from those spiritual practices.

2. Do you see yourself already growing in new areas? What form are these new patterns of spirituality already taking? In what ways might you intentionally develop these new areas further?

3. Think of one or two people whom you particularly like or admire for

their spiritual depth. Can you determine which patterns of spirituality they manifest most often? Think of one aspect of one of those patterns that you might like to try. Try to exercise that form of spirituality daily for a week, then reevaluate.

4. Think of one or two people in your congregation whom you find particularly irritating. See if you can determine which patterns of spirituality are most comfortable for them. It is possible that they engage in patterns of spirituality that are uncomfortable to you. Pick one aspect of an uncomfortable spirituality and try exercising it once a day for a week. Reevaluate at the end of the week.

Questions for congregational leaders:

1. You probably have places in your congregation to express many of the patterns of spirituality described in this chapter. Spend some time thanking God for the variety of places to serve and worship in your congregation. Thank God for the variety of people in your congregation and their diversity of gifts.

2. Consider all eight patterns of spirituality described in this chapter:

    a. *extraverted sensing.* In what ways in your congregation could you more often express joy in the wonders of creation? Enhance the physical environment in your congregation? Use your physical bodies?
    b. *introverted sensing.* In what ways could you do more to honor your congregational memories and nurture a sense of your history? Evaluate your use of traditions. In what ways could you encourage people to think, write, and meditate about their personal faith history?
    c. *extraverted intuition.* In what ways could you create more access for congregation members to be involved in vision setting and brainstorming? In what ways could you use symbolic rituals more effectively? How could you encourage prayers of hopeful anticipation?
    d. *introverted intuition.* In what ways could you encourage silent prayer and meditation? How could you do more to encourage meditation on the symbols, metaphors, and images of faith? How could

you do a better job of encouraging people with quiet insight to teach and lead?

e. *extraverted thinking.* In what ways could you provide opportunities for leadership, over both small and large events and programs, that encourages goal setting and effective implementation? In what ways could you affirm the benefits of well-run programs and clear communication about dates and plans? In what ways could you encourage discussion of questions and issues?

f. *introverted thinking.* In what ways could you encourage exploration and discussion of questions and issues? In what ways could you do a better job of affirming that questioning is a significant part of faith?

g. *extraverted feeling.* In what ways could you do a better job of providing opportunities to care for those in need? In what ways could you engage more people in praying for people in need? In what ways could you help people in caring ministries to do a better job of caring for themselves, too?

h. *introverted feeling.* In what ways could you create more opportunities for people to explore, discuss, and pray for their deeply held values? In what ways could you make a place for social activism?

3. Pick one or two of the eight patterns of spirituality that are not well represented in your congregation. Brainstorm with one or two other people some possibilities to make a way for expression of that form of spirituality.

CHAPTER 8

Clergy at Midlife

You search out my path and my lying down, and are acquainted with all my ways. Even before a word is on my tongue, O Lord, you know it completely.

Psalm 139:3, 4

Pastors, priests, and rabbis deal with the same kinds of issues at midlife that the members of their congregations face. Pastors, priests, and rabbis might have painful arguments with their teenage children. They might have to face the reality that they may never marry or have children. They might have parents who require help with complicated decisions about medical care.

Losses are probably piling up in their lives: loss of some of the hopes of young adulthood, loss of friends and family members to death, and loss of physical strength. Some members of the clergy face intense midlife crises, questioning their identity, their purpose in life, and their faith.

Most of the midlife stories recounted in this book could have come from the lips of clergy, who are, after all, human beings and encounter the same challenges, difficulties, and losses experienced by their congregation members. In addition to the issues of midlife already recounted in this book, clergy face specific questions and concerns that arise from the uniqueness of their jobs. In this chapter we will look at the unique challenges faced by clergy at midlife, along with a variety of prescriptions for health and wholeness.

Immunity to Midlife Turmoil

First and foremost, clergy face the challenge of the expectation that they are immune to midlife turmoil. This expectation may be rooted in the belief that clergy are more spiritual and thus they are—or should be—untouched by normal human pain. This myth asserts that true faith makes human beings such excellent people and such excellent parents that truly faithful people won't struggle with anything. Clergy par excellence are supposed to be full of true faith, so they simply shouldn't struggle very much in any area.

Presbyterian minister Kenneth Alan Moe describes 10 perils of parish ministry in his book *The Pastor's Survival Manual*. One of his perils is "unrealistic expectations," and he lists a dozen ways that congregation members commonly expect their pastors and pastors' families to be above human need and human weakness.[1] I have observed in myself the subtle temptation to believe these unrealistic expectations for myself.

Here's an example. A minister and his wife begin to experience strain as the empty nest approaches. Their marriage has always been difficult, and they know they will no longer have children to focus on. The minister knows he shouldn't share his painful, fearful feelings about his marriage with anyone in his congregation. He's been working so hard in recent years, giving his miniscule free time to his family, so he hasn't been able to develop many friendships outside his congregation. So where can he talk about these fearful feelings?

He has bought into the myth of pastoral perfection just enough to feel embarrassed to admit these fears, even to himself. To cover up the fears, he works even harder and tries to do a better job. This reduces his contact with friends outside the congregation even further. In addition, there is conflict in the congregation, which is enormously stressful to him because he always envisioned himself as the pastor of a thriving, healthy, happy congregation. He is caught in a cycle of perfectionism that he can't admit to anyone.

Any stressful event that happens during the midlife years can set off such a cycle. It might be a full-blown midlife crisis, full of pain and intense questions, but it could also be any accumulation of the typical losses that occur at midlife: the death of a friend, conflicts with teenagers, difficult decisions about aging parents, or any number of other situations. The cycle typically includes some amount of denial about the grief and loss the person is experiencing, coupled with some degree of unrealistic expectations about what a clergy person should experience.

As the cycle gets going, anything can happen. If the minister has unresolved issues regarding his sexuality, he might begin an inappropriately intimate friendship with a woman, or he might start a full-fledged affair. He might engage in other high-risk behavior. He might fall into depression.

He might desperately embrace anything and everything that can help him improve his ministry, trying out whatever latest and greatest idea he hears about. He might muddle along for years, doing his job but finding little joy in it. One Methodist minister told me she believes burned-out ministers kill churches, and that she has seen far too many examples of that form of slow death.

Bob, a presbytery executive—a pastor to pastors in the Presbyterian Church—told me he estimates three-quarters of the pastoral terminations he has witnessed over the years are related to midlife issues. Congregations have done virtually nothing to help their members understand midlife issues, he said, and that lack of attention backfires on clergy. Because midlife is seldom talked about, congregational leaders are unable to help their ministers and rabbis figure out strategies for coping with the unexpected emotions in the face of unexpected losses that are so common at midlife.

More Unrealistic Expectations

In addition to the unrealistic expectation that clergy will not experience normal human emotions, another set of expectations can contribute to midlife distress for clergy. These expectations are rooted in dreams and desires that date back to the early years of the career choice to enter seminary.

Bob, the presbytery executive mentioned above, describes these expectations. "In seminary, most people develop a picture of what they expect from ministry and what will be the marks of success. During their first 10 to 15 years, they feel optimism about reaching that vision. 'I truly can change the church,' they think. If they went to seminary in their 20s, they feel optimism well into their 30s, because they know there's still plenty of time to achieve their goals.

"But in their early 40s, they begin to experience the sense that the time is running out. 'I'm not doing anything I hoped to do,' they think. 'I thought I'd be the pastor of a 9,000-member church. I thought I would be serving the kind of vibrant church that becomes a model for the denomination.'

"When that dream crashes, there's a void left that is particularly difficult to fill. When people in a secular job experience the death of a dream, that's hard enough; but they have options for change. In fact, some of them go to seminary and become pastors! But clergy feel trapped because of their sense of call.

"They experience a ping pong match of emotions, ranging from profound anxiety to profound self-doubt. 'I'm 45,' they think. 'I'm not even a good pastor. What can I do for the rest of my life?'"

Mike, 53, is an Episcopal priest who worked as a flight instructor and owned a pest-control business in his 20s before going to seminary. He says, "What's going on at midlife is that we try to catch up on what we've missed, to live our unlived lives. This is particularly acute if there haven't been a variety of experiences in our 20s."

Mike has seen in himself and in others "a romantic, sentimental fantasy that we will find in the church a wonderful family that will be ours forever." The fantasy died for him, he says, as he learned the reality of what the church is truly like.

Mike and Bob agree that the clergy most at risk for a painful encounter with unrealistic expectations at midlife are those who had unrealistic goals when they chose to go into ministry as a career. They are more likely to be driven by the need for achievement and less likely to be in touch with their own spirituality or to be closely connected to colleagues.

Mike adds, "People who blow out the worst are those who have been the most narrowly focused."

Narrow Focus

Because most clergy are conscientious, hard-working people, their tendency in the face of stress is to work harder. Unfortunately, working harder throws their life even further out of balance and makes them even more narrowly focused.

One minister told me, "I knew when my life was out of balance. I started thinking about taking a sabbatical, and I couldn't think of anything I wanted to do with a year's worth of free time."

I have observed the same pattern in my own life. When I am working very hard, during a stretch of time (hopefully limited!) with lots of responsibilities, I begin to lose the ability to think of things to do in my time off. My focus is narrowed to the tasks at hand, and all I can think about is getting them finished. It is like an addiction or an obsession. And it is dangerous.

Table C

MYTHS THAT IMPACT CLERGY AT MIDLIFE

1. Clergy are immune from human need and weakness.
2. Clergy don't need rest.
3. If I'm under stress, the best idea is to work harder.
4. If there's conflict, I've done something wrong.
5. My congregation members need to take care of themselves at midlife, but I don't.

Alban Institute researcher and consultant Roy Oswald describes the rationale for embracing a balanced life in his book *Clergy Self-Care: Finding a Balance for Effective Ministry*. Oswald writes that because clergy are in the health and wholeness business, we need to be very conscious of the ways we embrace wholeness and balance for ourselves. "Who and what we are as persons is our most effective tool in pastoral ministry," he believes.[2] When our vision is so narrowly focused on our work, we not only become poor role models for congregation members, we also run the risk that our lack of balance will infect the whole congregational system.

Signs of narrowed focus include neglect of family, lack of friendships outside the congregation, few or no hobbies, and little time alone for reflection. As the stresses and issues of midlife arise, family and friends are essential because we need people to talk with. Hobbies and time alone are essential in order to have space and freshness for working through the questions of midlife.

Yet the tendency to work even harder when under stress narrows the focus and short-circuits the very habits that help us cope.

Those of us whose default mode is to work harder under stress need to examine carefully the forces inside us that are driving us to work so hard. Do we really believe that we are somehow different from normal human beings in that we don't really need rest? Do we believe that our call to ministry is so spiritually powerful that we lose all human weakness and need for balance and rest? Are we so indispensable to God that we must work all the time?

I see in myself the way that hard work can so easily become a form of idolatry. In order to resist it, I need to reaffirm my humanity and my limitations. God is God and I am not.

Conflict

Bob, the Presbytery executive mentioned above, has seen many pastors in their 40s derailed by conflict in their congregations. He says, "When you're in your 30s, conflict isn't so scary. There's time. 'I can always get another congregation,' you think. In your 40s, congregational conflict becomes much more scary because time is running out to achieve your dreams of success as a pastor. You find yourself thinking, 'What's the matter with me that I can't cope with this?'

"Conflict is very difficult for many clergy. They haven't come to terms with their tendency to idealize. They haven't come to understand that conflict is a part of human life."

The Lombard Mennonite Peace Center defines conflict as "differences that matter." Because God created each of us as unique human beings, there will always be differences that matter, even in heaven. Conflict can be constructive if it moves us in the direction of needed change in a way that minimizes hurt to people. Just like anger and fear, described in chapter 5, conflict can help us understand what is important to us.[3]

If ministers and rabbis haven't come to grips with the reality of conflict in congregational life by the time they reach midlife, and if they haven't learned some conflict management skills, they will probably face some significant problems in their congregations or in their personal lives. Inability to cope with conflict can throw clergy into the cycle of perfectionism and denial described earlier in the chapter.

Trapped by a Sense of Call

Many people respond to the revelations of midlife by making a career change. Often, clergy don't feel free to consider that option because they had, or have, such a strong sense of call to ministry.

That makes nurture and self-care for clergy at midlife even more significant. If we want to be faithful to what we believe we've been called to do, if we want to be effective in the long haul, we need to consider what will help us do that.

All of the suggestions in this book are relevant to clergy. Here's a list of just a few: Take time to journal and reflect on the losses that are becoming more real at midlife. Find new people to talk with. Explore new patterns of spirituality. Choose to take joy in the physical creation. Learn a new physical skill. Begin a new pattern of Sabbath observance. Create a place in your home or yard for meditation and prayer.

Many clergy will find a major obstacle to all of this midlife experimentation; they simply don't have time. We're back to the same issue described at the beginning of this chapter. Clergy so easily fall into the trap of believing that self-nurture is not as important for us as it is for other people. The sense of call to a spiritual ministry makes us immune to human weakness and human need.

Hopefully we can overcome that mythology and learn to take appropriate care of ourselves. In the rest of this chapter we will explore prescriptions for midlife health that are especially significant and helpful to clergy.

Developing Personal Spirituality

Every book I consulted on clergy self-care and clergy stress emphasized the importance of continuing to rediscover and develop our own personal spiritual lives. Every minister I interviewed emphasized the same thing. Because clergy spend their lives dealing with matters of faith, there is a constant temptation to believe that we are doing enough to develop our own spirituality. We may be aware that we have been organizing events, talking with others about their spiritual lives, and conducting worship so others can meet God. Still, it feels like we've been focused on God and faith, so it must be enough.

Roy Oswald writes, "The way to keep a congregation vital is to be a vital, growing person in their midst. Clergy don't need more knowledge or skills as much as they need a deeper spiritual life." Yet, he has observed, "Many clergy feel guilty for taking time for their own personal spiritual feeding; they regard it as selfish. They do not realize that, unless regular time is taken, they will not have the spiritual depth to sustain a healthy ministry."[4]

Joan, a Methodist minister, uses a booklet with her congregation that includes meditations and exercises centering around four questions: Who am I? What do I love? How should I live knowing I will die? What can I do to serve the earth? She finds she needs to be engaged in the same exercises and meditations in order to lead them effectively.

Rhoda, a Unitarian minister, says, "My social justice work has to be grounded in my spiritual practice. For me, that practice is Buddhist meditation. I have learned I must make a concerted effort to make time for it."

Joshua, a rabbi, affirms the importance for rabbis of "anything that connects us to God, to our inner being," which includes spiritual meditation, communal and personal prayer, attending services, learning and reading, and Sabbath observance.

One minister told me he has observed that the clergy who struggle the most in their 40s are the ones who are most out of touch with their own spirituality. They know how to look spiritual, he says, but there is no substance behind the appearance.

Midlife is often a time of developing new patterns of spirituality. Clergy should embrace this truth for their congregation members and for themselves. The options for experimentation are endless. Spend a few days at a monastery. When you work in the garden or take a walk, try to focus on the gift of God's creation. Try using candles or other physical objects to help you focus on God. If you have always studied the Bible in an analytical fashion, try some noncognitive meditative techniques using Scripture. Experiment with praying the Psalms. Read a book on prayer or meditation that comes from outside your tradition and experiment with some new patterns.

One minister developed a new pattern of daily devotions in his late 40s. "Always before, I tried to study the Bible and pray every morning," he says. "Prayer meant talking to God. Now I sit in the chapel every morning in silence. I try to allow enough time so that I can sit there until I receive the assurance that God loves me. I wait until I have that assurance. Prayer has changed for me. It is no longer just talking. It's listening."

New spiritual practices at midlife can be life changing. New honesty in prayer can also be vitally important.

Brutal Self-Honesty

Rod, 45, is a Presbyterian minister who has made an informal study of men who engage in high-risk behavior. He has observed a pattern of highly successful men who seem to need the adrenaline rush of the risk of self-destruction. He has seen businessmen and clergy alike who fall into this pattern.

He describes this pattern as rooted in the "physical longing for con-summation that never ends," an externalization of the need for intimacy. Men who fall into this pattern of risk, he observes, have usually spent very little energy on the cultivation of genuinely satisfying relationships, and they have usually failed to honestly face their own sexuality.

When a highly successful man begins to flirt with danger, seldom does anyone confront him. Successful people are cloaked in the assumption of trust that they know what they're doing. No one wants to interfere.

Close supportive relationships, with lots of accountability, can be help-ful. However, some of the men who endanger their careers with high-risk behavior have plenty of long-term friends. They are very successful at snow jobs with their friends; they have learned how to cover up what's really going on.

How then can we avoid falling into high-risk behavior under stress? Rod emphasizes that brutal self-honesty is the only answer. Each of us as individuals, he says, "has to face our own stuff."

Honesty in prayer was a significant aspect of healing and health at midlife for quite a few of the people I interviewed. No one else can deci-pher our lives for us. Only we can. Seeking the presence of the One who made us is one of the best arenas for attempting to do that.

Baptist minister Tony Pappas, in his book *Pastoral Stress*, uses the term "soulstress" to describe the kind of stress that infiltrates our inner being. One of his prescriptions for coping with soulstress is prayer. He writes,

> By prayer I do not mean a casual request for God's presence. I do not mean unilateral instructions directed to the divine. I do not mean a plea for relief. I mean rather a sincere opening of the heart and mind to the message God has placed within the soulstress. This prayer requires the belief that there is a blessing in the pain and confusion. That from the pain may come an impetus to change and from the confusion may come an insight into a deeper truth. It is an examination of the stress. An asking of why does this hurt. What is it within me that experiences this situation in this way?[5]

Pappas's last question is crucial. Something inside us causes us to react the way we do in every situation. We need to strive to understand the forces at work within us. Obviously, we can't understand everything, but at midlife some of our unconscious desires and longings will come to the surface. We need to be prepared to spend the time and energy it takes to explore them. Otherwise we will probably fall into counterproductive, unhealthy behavior.

It is only by brutal honesty with ourselves in the presence of God that we can avoid the kind of denial that leads us to do stupid things in the face of our own stress and overload. It is only God who can meet us and give us true encouragement in the pain of unfulfilled dreams and expectations. Just because we have been ordained or set apart for God's service doesn't mean that we don't have to continue to draw near to God.

It will be out of a deep personal honesty with God that we will discover exactly what it looks like for us, personally and individually, to be faithful and responsible. This is an ongoing, lifelong process that requires continuous exercise of spiritual disciplines. We can't settle the issue of personal call—or any of the other issues that face us—once for all.

Meeting regularly with a therapist or a spiritual director can help encourage self-honesty, as can a support group committed to exercise accountability. But either of those can become a crutch. We may find ourselves thinking, "I have a support group. They're holding me accountable, so I'm doing okay." Ultimately we stand alone before God, accountable for our actions.

Remembering the First Love

Rhoda, 43, is a Unitarian Universalist minister whose story illustrates two other important prescriptions for health at midlife for clergy. Rhoda is the only pastor of a booming church of 450 people. She has been ordained for 12 years and has served her current church for seven years. About a year ago she found herself exhausted and overwhelmed. She realized, "I couldn't put my finger on what was wrong, but I felt like I'd been spinning my wheels for more than a year, that I had lost my focus. I'd fallen into the trap that so many ministers fall into—working harder and harder because things were going well."

The great love of Rhoda's early adult life was social justice. She was an activist for many causes and derived great energy from her social justice work. After her ordination, she continued to be involved in social causes. It was only the birth of her first child six years ago that slowed down her activism.

"I became an organizer rather than an activist," she reflects. "I preached about social justice rather than being involved in it myself."

Rhoda decided to attend a program called "Sojourners" at the Center for Career Development in Ministry in Massachusetts.[6] The program, two days of intensive counseling, is designed for ministers who are not in crisis but who need to refocus. Rhoda came up with a long-range plan for her ministry.

She says, "The plan helped me realize that in order for me to be happy in ministry, social justice needs to be front and center. I came back to the church and initiated a five-year planning process with an outside consultant. We looked at 12 areas of ministry. With the leaders of the congregation, I picked five areas that I would focus on. I simply won't be involved in the other seven areas. If I'm going to be in ministry for the long haul, I have to be clear on what my ministry is about, and I have to be clear with the congregation regarding what I can and cannot do."

Rhoda realizes that because she has children at home, she will not be able to do as much social activism as she did in her 20s, but she is still committed to incorporating more of it into her life and ministry. She is also exploring ways she can be involved in social ministries with her children.

Establishing Priorities

When Rhoda and her congregational leaders met with the outside consultant and established priorities for Rhoda's ministry and for the congregation as a whole, she was embracing another important prescription for health in her ministry. She was consciously choosing what to do and what not to do.

When I look back on my 20s, I realize that I was able to tackle just about everything that came along. With each passing year, there is an accumulation of relationships and responsibilities. By midlife, the accumulation is too heavy to carry without some careful weeding out. Just about everyone at midlife needs to do some careful discerning and weeding, and clergy are not immune from that need.

In *Pastoral Stress* Pappas lists 10 models for ministry. Pastoral work is multifaceted, he acknowledges, which means that any minister or rabbi will certainly work out of more than one model. But it is impossible to work out of all 10 models. Clergy need to clarify in their own minds and with their congregational leaders which of the models are most important to them and which will be consciously neglected.

Here are the 10 models:

- Counselor/Healer/Caretaker
- Minister of the Word
- Administrator/Manager of an Organization
- Prophet/Social Activist
- Social Exemplar
- Ring Leader
- Community Personage
- Celebrant
- Spiritual Guide
- Witness[7]

This list may be helpful in weeding out what is least important to the minister or rabbi and to the congregation.

Trying New Things

Almost every minister and rabbi I interviewed talked about the challenge of staying fresh, and almost all of them mentioned that they consciously try to experiment with new areas of ministry. Joan, 54, a Methodist minister, says, "I try to always be working on one thing where I'm stretching, growing, learning. I talk to people about that area. I experiment."

Right now Joan is focusing on volunteers, helping people in her congregation to find their calling and trying to nurture and support people who are already volunteering. She has read books to get ideas. She brought in a national consultant to do a conference at her church on recruiting and caring for volunteers. She is enthusiastic and excited when she talks about what she's been learning.

Joshua, a rabbi in his early 50s, reflects, "Burnout is common at midlife because the job is so demanding. Rabbis after 50 tend to stay in the same congregation because it's hard to move. The pro of staying is that continuity is good. The con is that it's easy to lose freshness. I always make an effort to try new things and talk with people about new ideas." For health at midlife, Joshua emphasizes some of the same things already discussed in this chapter: "In any giving profession, there needs to be frequent soul searching. There needs to be conscious development of personal spirituality."

Combining These Suggestions: Study Leave

Three of the suggestions mentioned in this chapter might seem to be in conflict with each other: remembering our first love, establishing priorities, and trying new things. The three need to be held in tension. We can't go around trying so many new things that we have no priorities at all or that we forget the first love that brought us into ministry. We can't be so focused on our first love that we neglect to establish priorities that are appropriate for today and neglect to stay fresh by experimenting with new ideas and new ways of doing things.

These three suggestions—remembering our first love, establishing priorities, and trying new things—plus the need to develop our personal spiritual disciplines, need to shape choices for study leave during the midlife years. If you habitually use your study leave to explore new skills for ministry, maybe it's time to focus your study leave on something you used to love but haven't spent much time on lately. If you always attend the same conference during your study leave, maybe it's time to try something new, particularly something focused on a new skill you would like to develop. Maybe it's time to use study leave for a conference that would help you establish priorities in your ministry.

Perhaps the most valuable use of study leave would be to spend a whole week focusing on personal spirituality. A guided silent retreat can teach skills for spiritual practice as well as giving many hours for reflection and prayer. A conference on contemplative prayer or meditation techniques could give a jump-start on spiritual practice for the next year.

Kyle, 44, is allotted two weeks of study leave each year, and he always spends them the same way. In the spring he spends a week with another youth pastor. They go to a cabin in the woods, and Kyle uses the week to plan the June youth outreach trip to Mexico. He writes Bible study questions and plans activities. He spends a few hours each day reading books that he has saved up all year to read.

In the fall he attends a national convention of youth workers. Last year he took along six of the adults who work with youth in his congregation. He was thrilled to have them there for the conference, but it certainly changed his experience of the week.

Kyle is experiencing the "blahs" in his ministry. Nothing seems fresh anymore. Is he getting too old for youth work? He wonders what else could he do.

Before Kyle makes any decisions about his career, he should carefully consider the way he uses his study leave. Planning events is essential, but it should not be considered study leave. Taking a group of youth leaders to a conference is a wonderful thing, but it should not be counted as study leave for the pastor who takes them. Last year Kyle really had only one or two days of true study leave: the hours he spent reading at the cabin.

Even if no youth workers come with Kyle next year to the national convention, Kyle should consider new ways of using his study leave. He may benefit most from attending a conference that would help him discover his personal priorities for ministry, or he might need most a place where he can spend a lot of time in prayer and hear God's voice afresh. Or maybe he should attend a conference on some aspect of ministry that has nothing to do with youth work.

Maybe he should consider leaving his job, but maybe not. Putting some careful thought into the way he uses his study leave would be a helpful first step.

Considering Leaving the Ministry

Gil was one of those people who could not imagine doing anything other than being a pastor. He was active in leadership in his church as a teenager. After high school, he went into the Army, where he led Bible studies with the chaplain. He went to college and seminary on the G.I. bill and became a Methodist minister at 30.

In his late 30s Gil was serving a church in Chicago and became active in housing ministries. He found himself more and more absorbed in issues regarding housing, but he was unwilling to consider leaving his pastorate. He had been involved in ministry since he was a teenager. It was the only thing he knew how to do, and he had no idea what else he could do. In fact, he was terrified of doing anything else.

But the interest in housing issues continued to grow, while his dissatisfaction with parish ministry increased alongside. At 40, he left his parish and got a graduate degree in public administration. Now, six years later, he is a national consultant in the area of public housing. He has more energy in his 40s than he had in his 30s. He loves what he is doing, and he is certain he made the right decision. But he acknowledges that it was a wrenching experience to leave pastoral ministry. He had to reframe his sense of call to ministry to include secular work, and that was not easy.

For every person who leaves a secular job to go to seminary, maybe there should be another person who leaves ministry to go into a secular job. At the very least, we need to recognize that the midlife drive to discover who we really are and the equal drive to try new things will surely lead a good number of ministers and rabbis into new fields.

Some Unusual Situations

What about those people who begin their career in ministry during the midlife years. Are they immune to midlife struggling? Yes and no.

Joan, 54, became a minister in her early 40s after several different careers. She was used to frequent job changes, so it seemed natural, after four years in her first parish, to move to another. Now she has been in one place for six years, and she feels a deep need for change and variety. She tries to meet that need by focusing on new areas of ministry.

"I don't have midlife issues," she says. "My restlessness comes from mid-career questions, not midlife questions." Surely there is much overlap between the two.

A related question, which is largely unanswered, is whether women who begin a career in ministry during their 20s face the same midlife issues that male clergy face. Do they experience some of the same devastating loss of dreams of success? Do they experience the same unrealistic expectations of themselves as clergy? As more women have long careers in ministry, these questions will be answered.

Congregations Supporting Clergy

Congregations can help their pastors and rabbis navigate midlife by providing support in several areas. First, they can work hard to revise their own expectations that clergy should be superhuman. They can try to understand that all human beings, including clergy, face transitions in life, and that many significant transitions happen during the midlife years.

Congregational leaders can help clergy set priorities by being open to the idea that one person can't do everything. If the minister or rabbi initiates a planning and prioritization process, congregational leaders can be supportive by welcoming such a discussion and by including in the discussion a time to discuss the priorities for the minister or rabbi. If congregational leaders sense that the minister or rabbi is consistently overloaded, they can initiate some discussion about priorities.

Congregational leaders can help hold clergy accountable for wise use of study leave. Personnel committee members and congregational board members may feel reluctant to push their ministers or rabbis very hard about their study leave, but asking some hard questions about study leave may be a very supportive action.

Bob, the presbytery executive mentioned above, believes that all ministers should take a sabbatical sometime in their 40s. He believes that church governing bodies should require it. In the absence of such a requirement, congregations can offer the option of a sabbatical to ministers and rabbis in their 40s.

Bob remembers the way a personnel committee chair provided support for him at one of the churches he served early in his ministry. This story illustrates very well the spirit of support that congregational leaders can provide for their ministers and rabbis.

The chair of the personnel committee had an arrangement with Bob. If she left a plate of cookies on his desk, it was his responsibility to call her within 24 hours. The conversations typically went something like this.

"I noticed you had two funerals last week," she would say. "And they weren't your typical funerals. One of them was for a suicide victim. You've been looking very tired and stressed out since last week. What are you going to do about it? Could you take some time to get together with your minister's support group? Could you go see your counselor? Could you take a day off?"

She stayed on the phone until he told her what he was going to do to nurture himself in the midst of his stress. Then she would call back a week later to check to see that he had followed through.

She didn't say, "How can I pray for you?" or "How can I help you?" She simply asked him what he intended to do to take care of himself, and she provided accountability to help him follow through.

Too often congregational leaders fall into one or the other extreme. Either they ignore the personal needs of their ministers and rabbis or they try to meet those personal needs themselves. This woman had the right balance. She helped Bob see that his stress and overload were visible and therefore action was needed. She made it clear that she wasn't going to leave him alone until he took some action. But she left it up to him to find the support he needed.

That is the appropriate spirit of support and accountability that clergy need from their congregational leaders. Midlife issues are real, and clergy need encouragement to figure out how they can best address those issues.

The Call to Faithfulness

Bob says, "The midlife shift puts us in touch with our call to be faithful. We are not called to change the world, just to be faithful. At 40, we may not know exactly what it means to be faithful, but we recognize that we will probably have 40 more years to work towards it. So we need to figure out what it means."

Through wise use of study leave, through careful development of our own personal spirituality, through wise setting and keeping of priorities we can work towards a clearer understanding of what it means to be faithful in clergy roles.

Questions for Reflection

For clergy:

1. Look at table C, "Myths that Impact Clergy at Midlife," on page 136. In what ways do those myths impact your life and ministry? What could you do to refute those myths?

2. Look over the following list of common clergy problems at midlife. In what ways do these affect your life and ministry?

    * unrealistic expectations
    * narrow focus
    * trapped by a sense of call
    * unable to deal constructively with conflict

3. What would it look like for you to nurture your own personal spirituality more intentionally? What are the obstacles? What would it look like for you to set clearer priorities for your life and ministry?

4. Consider the tension between the issue of remembering your first love and learning new skills. Do you spend too much time on one of these two? In what ways could you embrace both of them more effectively?

5. Make a list of what you have done with your study leave for the past five years. Analyze this list, looking for these four components:

    -   your first love
    -   new skills
    -   setting priorities
    -   developing personal spirituality

    Consider ways your study leave could incorporate one or more of these four aspects more effectively.

6. Consider the ways you receive support outside your congregation. What could you do to develop these support structures further?

For congregations supporting clergy at midlife:

1. In what ways do you not allow your pastor or rabbi to be human?

2. In what ways could you do a better job affirming your pastor or rabbi's need to establish and live by priorities for ministry?

3. In what ways could you give your minister or rabbi more feedback and accountability regarding study leave?

4. Consider establishing a policy regarding sabbaticals for your clergy.

Practical Ideas for Becoming a Midlife-Friendly Congregation

Compiled here are lists of all the practical suggestions for congregations mentioned in this book, arranged topically so that you can discuss them and consider whether and how to implement some of them.

Making Space for God

Encourage noncognitive meditation on Scripture.
Encourage praying the Psalms.
Encourage the quiet activities of faith and the journey inward.
Unashamedly promote the exercise of spiritual disciplines such as daily prayer and meditation, attendance at worship, and commitment to service.
Establish simplicity circles.
Encourage Sabbath observance.
Take a group to a monastery for a few days.

Topics for Seminars and Classes

Midlife
Simplicity
Money
Work
Sex
Assertiveness
Conflict Management

How to Journal
How to Pray and/or Meditate
Contemplative Prayer
Discovering Your Gifts/How to Find a Place to Serve
Explore What You Believe/Telling Faith Stories
Grief/How to Care for People Who Are Grieving
Preparing for Your Own Death
Inner Healing/Healing of Past Wounds
Marriage Enrichment

Topics for Seminars and Classes for Parents

Parenting Adolescents
Talking with Teens about Sex
Creative Ways to Engage Children in Sabbath Observance
A Class on the Book *Reviving Ophelia: Saving the Lives of
Adolescent Girls* by Mary Pipher

Structuring Seminars and Classes

Include significant opportunities for sharing, writing, and/or reflection.
Affirm honesty, questioning, being "real."
In classes for parents, provide time for them to reflect on what is
happening in their lives as they parent. What issues are being
raised?
Allow time for "life review."

In Small Groups

Provide a place to be honest.
Work through conflict; don't ignore it.
Ask for help from clergy or congregational leaders when there is
conflict.
Provide practical support for people in grief.
Provide a listening ear to singles, infertile couples, parents of teens,
and others who are facing difficult issues.

In Sermons

Be "real."

Discuss rest and Sabbath observance.

Discuss work and its purpose.

Discuss the reality of conflict.

Affirm the positive role of anger.

Discuss sex.

Give positive pictures of aging, such as stories of older people growing, serving.

Tell stories about people who have endured deeply painful situations.

For Congregation Leaders

Be "real." Encourage people to honestly face the horrors and loneliness within them.

Affirm the place of anger in the great social movements of history.

Affirm the necessity of conflict.

Affirm the significance of the quiet inner life of faith as well as activities, service, witness.

Encourage people to try new areas of service.

Give people the freedom to quit serving.

Affirming Our Connection to the Creation

Use flowers and other natural decorations.

Display art in the building.

Hold a lecture series on scientific discoveries.

Sponsor a bike trip, hike, bird-watching expedition, or camping trip.

Hold summer services outside.

Encourage meditation on breath and light.

Use food to connect with history, such as at Passover and Purim.

Sponsor yoga or exercise classes.

Hire a parish nurse.

Hold a health fair.

Have a regular healing service.

Have a night of dancing, such as line dancing or contra dancing.

Host a Weigh Down class.

In Your Newsletter

Highlight the needs of the developing world.
Discuss patterns of Sabbath observance.
Provide a list of community resources that support marriages.
Provide positive models and stories of aging.
Provide resources for recovery and referrals to counselors.

Other Ideas

Use speakers, displays, and fund-raising efforts to present the needs of the developing world.
Sponsor trips to other countries.
Hold a work fair.
Sponsor Twelve Step groups.
Sponsor abuse recovery groups.
Begin an inner healing ministry.
Make a way for single people to connect with others at the holidays.
Don't use the word "family" unless you really mean that only families are welcome.
Plan intergenerational events rather than family events.
Start a marriage mentoring program.
Publicize marriage enrichment events in the community.
Be sensitive to couples battling infertility.
Provide practical help to people who are grieving.
Establish a Stephen Ministry or a similar program that provides a listening ear.
Make a way for men to serve in areas traditionally filled by women: cooking, providing practical care for people in need.

Practical Ideas Related to the Eight Patterns of Spirituality

Extraverted Sensing

Celebrate eating, dancing, hugs, Passover meals, and communion.
Use banners and seasonal decorations.
Use attractive design in printed materials and in your use of physical space.

Introverted Sensing

Embrace traditions and creeds.
Record and celebrate congregational history.
Make a way for people to explore their own personal faith history.

Extraverted Intuition

Use symbolic rituals, such as writing negative thoughts on paper and
then burning it.
Nurture prayer of hopeful anticipation.
Make a way for congregational involvement in setting vision.

Introverted Intuition

Encourage silent prayer and meditation.
Use images and metaphors in congregational prayers and in sermons.
Encourage people with quiet insight to lead and teach.

Extraverted Thinking

In classes and seminars, allow time for discussion and encourage
questions.
Be clear in your communication of dates and future plans.
Affirm the way a smoothly run event honors the people involved.

Introverted Thinking

Encourage questions about faith, meaning, and all aspects of life.
Encourage expression of a passion for truth and justice.

Extraverted Feeling

Provide practical help to people in need.
Provide a place for people to pray for those in need, such as a prayer
chain.
Enable congregational leaders to say no, to stop serving, and to rest.

Introverted Feeling

> Make a place for people to explore their values.
> Encourage prayer for peace, justice, racial reconciliation.
> Make a place for social activism.

A Class or Seminar on Midlife

To adapt the material in this book for a class or seminar, the first issue to explore is the total length of time available. For a class of three or four sessions, or for a seminar of three to four hours, you would be wise to limit yourself to the material in the first three or four chapters.

The personal reflection questions at the end of each chapter can be used for small group discussion or personal journaling in a class or seminar. I have never experienced any trouble getting people to talk about their midlife experiences; the challenge is to consider the purpose you desire in having people share. Is your primary purpose for people not to feel alone in their struggles with midlife issues? Do you want to provide encouragement for movement in a certain direction? Choose discussion questions based on your purposes in sharing.

A nonverbal component is very helpful in discussing midlife issues. At the first seminar I attended on midlife spirituality, the presenters spread a collection of about 100 art-print postcards on a table. Participants were asked to pick three cards (which they were expected to return at the end of the session). These were the specific instructions: "Pick three cards that you have a connection with, or that repel you, or let the cards choose you. Write about how each one illustrates your past, present, or future journey."

I have begun a collection of photographs cut out of magazines. I choose photos of plants, flowers, animals, landscapes, and people, aiming for a collection that captures a wide variety of moods and activities. I use the photographs in seminars on midlife. Here are my instructions: "Pick two photographs. Pick one that represents something about what you are currently experiencing in your midlife journey. Pick a second one that represents something about where you are headed or where you would like to be headed." I ask participants to share in small groups about the pictures they have chosen or to write about them.

Another way to access some of the non-verbal issues around midlife is to give each person a stick of clay and ask them to fashion something out of the clay that represents their midlife journey.

A Three-Hour Seminar on Midlife

1. Opening presentation: 30 minutes covering material from chapter one and two, beginning with metaphors for midlife, and then briefly covering messengers of midlife, biological changes, and the male-female flip-flop. Give an overview of the spiritual issues of midlife, using a handout or overhead that presents this list of issues:

   - the drive to discover deeply held values
   - the call to meaningful service
   - the joy of simplicity
   - the need for "alone" time
   - facing the reality of death
   - letting go of the illusion of control
   - growing ability to live with ambiguity
   - greater sense of mystery and awe
   - new views of God
   - facing old wounds and receiving healing
   - finding God in expressions of creativity

2. Small groups of four to six people: 30 minutes. Focus: Your experiences of midlife. I like to give people the option to discuss midlife in same-sex groups or mixed groups. Discussion questions could include:

   a. What "messengers of midlife" are you experiencing? What impact have they had in your everyday life? In what ways have they drawn you closer to God? In what ways have they caused you to pull away from God?

   b. As you look over the list of "spiritual issues at midlife," which one or ones have you experienced the most intensely? How have you responded? Are there other spiritual issues that have arisen for you at midlife?

3. Large group discussion: 15 minutes. Ask people to share insights from their small groups or other thoughts about the list of spiritual issues at midlife.

4. Break for 15 minutes.

5. Reflection on photographs clipped from magazines: 20 minutes. Spread out photographs on large tables and ask participants to choose two photographs, one that speaks to them about their present experience of midlife, and the other that speaks to them about their hopes for the future. Ask them to write for 10 minutes about what the photographs say to them.

6. Allow 10 to 20 minutes for people to share in the large group about what the experience with the photographs meant to them.

7. Presentation: 30 minutes. Pick several of the spiritual issues of midlife to talk about in more depth, perhaps in response to what people have shared. You could also use some of the material from chapter 3 about family issues at midlife or chapter 4 about the paradoxes we experience at midlife.

8. Sharing in the same small groups: 15 to 25 minutes. Focus: Spiritual practices that work for each person. Questions could include:

   a. What gives you hope for the future? Which spiritual practices help you access hope?
   b. Many people experience a turn inward at midlife. Where do you find spaces in your life for reflection? Which spiritual practices have helped you reflect, meditate, and pray about your life?
   c. Which family issues are most real to you in these midlife years? Which spiritual practices have helped you find strength and peace in the midst of them?

9. Large group wrap-up: Five minutes. Close with the one idea that you consider to be the most important of all the material.

For Further Reading

Books on Midlife

Brehony, Kathleen A. *Awakening at Midlife: A Guide to Reviving Your Spirit, Recreating Your Life, and Returning to Your Truest Self.* New York: Riverhead Books, 1996.
Written by a Jungian-oriented psychotherapist.

Carroll, L. Patrick, and Katherine Marie Dyckman. *Chaos or Creation: Spirituality in Mid-Life.* New York: Paulist Press, 1986.
Written by two Catholic writers, the book draws heavily on psychologists such as Carl Jung, Erik Erickson, and James Fowler.

Corlett, Eleanor S., and Nancy B. Millner. *Navigating Midlife: Using Typology as a Guide.* Palo Alto, Calif.: CPP Books, 1993.
Explores midlife patterns and issues for each of the 16 psychological types.

Cramer, Kathryn D. *Roads Home: Seven Pathways to Midlife Wisdom.* New York: William Morrow, 1995.
One of the seven pathways is "spiritual serenity."

Harnish, James A. *Men at Mid-Life: Steering Through the Detours.* Nashville: Dimensions for Living, 1993.
Written by a Methodist minister for men experiencing midlife upheaval and the women who are trying to support them.

Rupp, Joyce. *Dear Heart, Come Home: The Path of Midlife Spirituality.* New York: Crossroad Books, 1997.
Midlife spirituality from a Christian viewpoint, including topics of darkness, interiority, searching, grief, prayer, transformation, and healing.

Schachter-Shalomi, Zalman, and Ronald S. Miller. *From Age-ing to Sage-ing: A Profound New Vision of Growing Older.* New York: Warner Books, 1995.
A rabbi presents a picture of aging as a process of becoming an "elder," with positive challenges and new roles to fill.

Sheehy, Gail. *New Passages: Mapping Your Life Across Time.* New York: Ballantine Books, 1995.
Great stories from interviews with men and women in their forties, fifties, and sixties. Very little emphasis on spirituality, but still the must-read book on midlife.

Sheehy, Gail. *Understanding Men's Passages: Discovering the New Map of Men's Lives.* New York: Random House, 1998.
Focused on the forties, fifties, and sixties, with lots of material on sexual issues for men as they age.

Topics Related to Midlife

Broyles, Anne. *Journaling: A Spirit Journey.* Nashville: The Upper Room, 1988.
Ideas for journaling in response to life events, Scripture, guided meditations, dreams, and reading.

James, John W., and Russell Friedman. *The Grief Recovery Handbook: The Action Program for Moving Beyond Death, Divorce, and Other Losses.* New York: Harper Perennial, 1998.
Lots of practical ideas for processing many kinds of grief and loss. Includes helpful rituals.

Kelsey, Morton. *Adventure Inward: Christian Growth through Personal Journal Writing.* Minneapolis: Augsburg, 1980.
Presents the wide variety of spiritual issues that can be explored through journaling, with practical ideas.

Kise, Jane A. G., David Stark, and Sandra Krebs Hirsh. *Life Keys: Discovering Who You Are, Why You're Here, and What You Do Best.* Minneapolis: Bethany House, 1996.
Practical help in finding a place to serve by exploring spiritual gifts, personality type, values, and passions. An edition for teenagers has also been

published: *Find Your Fit* by Jane Kise and Kevin Johnson (Minneapolis: Bethany House, 1998).

Lerner, Harriet Goldhor. *The Dance of Anger*. New York: Harper and Row, 1985.
Explores the role of anger in relationships, with particular emphasis on on-going patterns.

Lindbergh, Anne Morrow. *Gift from the Sea*. New York: Random House, 1955 and 1978.
A classic. The first-person story of a woman slowing down and finding the inner resources to live with joy and peace.

Louden, Jennifer. *The Woman's Retreat Book*. New York: Harper San Francisco, 1997.
Lots of practical ideas for personal retreats, whether for an hour, a day, or a weekend.

Naylor, Thomas H., William H. Willimon, and Magdalena R. Naylor. *The Search for Meaning*. Nashville: Abingdon, 1994.
Describes the pervasive longing for meaning in today's culture and discusses issues revolving around the search for meaning, such as possessions, community, and work.

Steinberg, Laurence. *Crossing Paths: How Your Child's Adolescence Triggers Your Own Crisis*. New York: Simon and Schuster, 1994.
A fascinating presentation of the results of many interviews of parents of adolescents.

Tavris, Carol. *Anger: The Misunderstood Emotion*. New York: Simon and Schuster, 1982.
Explodes several common myths about anger and presents the positive and necessary aspects of anger.

Zweig, Connie, and Jeremiah Abrams, eds. *Meeting the Shadow: The Hidden Power of the Dark Side of Human Nature*. New York: Putnam and Sons, 1991.
Sixty-five well-chosen essays and book excerpts on the shadow. Considering the complexity of the topic, most are clear and easy to understand.

Exploring Spirituality

The Bible, in any contemporary translation.
We are in danger of forgetting this central resource for the spiritual journey.
The wide variety of human emotions in the Psalms, the passion for God in
the prophets, and the human frailty portrayed in the narrative passages can
be anchors in midlife. The enigmatic and subtle character of Jesus' parables
can be a powerful call to midlife creativity.

Brussat, Frederic, and Mary Ann Brussat. *Spiritual Literacy: Reading
the Sacred in Everyday Life*. New York: Scribner, 1996.
A large compendium of short readings on many topics related to spirituality,
taken from many of the world's religions.

de Mello, Anthony. *Sadhana, A Way to God: Christian Exercises in East-
ern Form*. New York: Doubleday, 1978.
Lots of meditative exercises are described in a practical way.

de Waal, Esther. *The Celtic Way of Prayer: The Recovery of the Religious Imagination*. New York: Doubleday, 1997.
An exploration of the major themes of Celtic Christian spirituality, with quo-
tations from many Celtic poems and songs.

Mirel, James L., and Karen Bonnel Werth. *Stepping Stones to Jewish
Spiritual Living*. Woodstock, Vt.: Jewish Lights Publishing, 1998.
Lots of practical ideas for meditations at different times during the day,
based on traditional Jewish practices.

Moore, Thomas. *Care of the Soul: A Guide for Cultivating Depth and
Sacredness in Everyday Life*. New York: Harper Collins, 1992.
Explores ways to rediscover our soul, to nurture that place inside us that
longs to connect with the transcendent.

Norris, Kathleen. *The Cloister Walk*. New York: Riverhead Books, 1996.
Essays on the Christian year in the context of the author's frequent resi-
dency in a Benedictine community.

Exploring Creativity

Cameron, Julia. *The Artist's Way: A Spiritual Path to Higher Creativity.*
New York: G. P. Putnam's Sons, 1992.
Presents a wide variety of practical ways to explore creativity, and links
creativity to developing a sense of compassion, identity, possibility, abundance, and faith.

Forbes, Cheryl. *Imagination: Embracing a Theology of Wonder.* Portland, Ore.: Multnomah Press, 1986.
A wonderfully inspiring exploration of the ways Christian faith and love are
nurtured by developing our ability to imagine.

Goldberg, Natalie. *Wild Mind: Living the Writer's Life.* New York: Bantam Books, 1990.
Full of very creative and interesting writing exercises, which could also be
used as discussion topics for a group.

The Basics of Personality Type

Hirsh, Sandra, and Jean Kummerow. *Life Types.* New York: Warner Books,
1989.

Kroeger, Otto, and Janet Thuesen. *Type Talk.* New York: Dell Publishing,
1988.

Myers, Isabel Briggs. *Gifts Differing.* Palo Alto, Calif.: Consulting Psychologists Press, 1980.

Pearman, Roger R., and Sarah C. Albritton. *I'm Not Crazy, I'm Just Not
You.* Palo Alto, Calif.: Davies Black Publishing, 1987.

Personality Type and Spirituality

Baab, Lynne M. *Personality Type in Congregations: How to Work with
Others More Effectively.* Bethesda, Md.: The Alban Institute, 1998.
Explores the variety of ways personality type can be used in congregations.

Duncan, Bruce. *Pray Your Way: Your Personality and God.* London: Darton, Longman, and Todd, 1993. (Distributed in the United States by Abingdon Press.)
Connects personality type and patterns of prayer.

Harbaugh, Gary L. *God's Gifted People: Discovering Your Personality as a Gift.* Minneapolis: Augsburg, 1988.
Describes common patterns of service based on personality type.

Hirsh, Sandra Krebs, and Jane A. G. Kise. *Looking at Type and Spirituality.* Gainesville, Fla.: Center for Applications of Psychological Type, 1997.
In the format of a large booklet, explores patterns of spirituality for the 16 types.

Hirsh, Sandra Krebs, and Jane A. G. Kise. *Soul Types: Finding the Spiritual Path That Is Right for You.* New York: Hyperion, 1998.
Explores patterns of spirituality for the 16 types, with lots of examples and stories from extensive interviews.

Johnson, Reginald. *Your Personality and God.* Wheaton, Ill.: Victor Books, 1988. (Originally published with the title *Celebrate My Soul.*)
Links personality type and patterns of spirituality, with illustrations of biblical characters.

For Clergy

Moe, Kenneth Alan. *The Pastor's Survival Manual: Ten Perils in Parish Ministry and How to Handle Them.* Bethesda, Md.: The Alban Institute, 1995.
Each of the 10 perils is presented clearly with practical suggestions.

Oswald, Roy. *Clergy Self-Care: Finding a Balance for Effective Ministry.* Washington, D.C.: The Alban Institute, 1991.
A comprehensive and wholistic presentation of ways clergy can remain emotionally and spiritually healthy in the midst of caring for a congregation.

Pappas, Anthony G. *Pastoral Stress: Sources of Tension, Resources for Transformation.* Bethesda, Md.: The Alban Institute, 1995.
Discusses sources of interpersonal, role-related, and congregational stress with suggestions for coping and thriving.

NOTES

Preface

1. Thad Rutter, Jr., *Where the Heart Longs to Go: A New Image for Pastoral Ministry* (Nashville: Upper Room Books, 1998).

2. Several studies are cited by Claudia Kalb in "Pen, Paper, Power," *Newsweek*, April 26, 1999.

Chapter 1

1. Eleanor S. Corlett and Nancy B. Millner, *Navigating Midlife: Using Typology as a Guide* (Palo Alto, Calif.: CPP Books, 1993), 1.

2. Joyce Rupp, *Dear Heart, Come Home: The Path of Midlife Spirituality* (New York: Crossroads Books, 1997), 16.

3. Gail Sheehy, *Understanding Men's Passages* (New York: Random House, 1998), 185, 186.

4. Sheehy was interviewed by Tim Madigan for *The Seattle Times* ("Men must reinvent themselves to survive midlife crisis," May 31, 1998) when she was in Seattle promoting *Understanding Men's Passages*. She expressed these recommendations in the interview.

5. Sheehy, *Understanding Men's Passages*, 177 ff.

6. Sheehy, *New Passages: Mapping Your Life Across Time* (New York: Ballantine, 1995), 320.

7. Sheehy, *New Passages*, 11.

8. Anne Morrow Lindbergh, *Gift From the Sea* (New York: Random House, 1955, 1978), 54, 55.

9. Rupp, *Dear Heart, Come Home*, 30.

10. James Harnish, *Men at Mid-Life: Steering Through the Detours* (Nashville: Dimensions for Living, 1993), 12.

11. Harnish, *Men at Mid-Life*, 12.

Chapter 2

1. David Briggs, "Middle Age Can Reveal Spiritual Need," *Minneapolis StarTribune*, June 20, 1998.

2. In *Stepping Stones to Jewish Spiritual Living*, the authors, Rabbi James L. Mirel and Karen Bonnell Werth, present a wide variety of meditative prayers based on

traditional Jewish practices such as hand-washing, hospitality, study of the Torah, and Sabbath observance. (Woodstock, Vt.: Jewish Lights Publishing, 1998.)

3. Thomas H. Naylor, William H. Willimon, and Magdalena R. Naylor, *The Search for Meaning* (Nashville: Abingdon, 1994), 27.

Chapter 3

1. Laurence Steinberg, *Crossing Paths: How Your Child's Adolescence Triggers Your Own Crisis* (New York: Simon and Schuster, 1994), 70, 71.

2. Steinberg, *Crossing Paths*, 70, 71.

3. Steinberg, *Crossing Paths*, 80-82.

4. Steinberg, *Crossing Paths*, 98-114.

5. Steinberg, *Crossing Paths*, 80-85. 91-93.

6. Steinberg, *Crossing Paths*, 62, 63.

7. Steinberg, *Crossing Paths*, 256.

8. Steinberg, *Crossing Paths*, 18.

9. Les and Leslie Parrott have written a very helpful little book for those who want to start a marriage mentoring program in their congregation: *The Marriage Mentor Manual* (Grand Rapids, Mich.: Zondervan, 1995).

Chapter 4

1. Rabbi James L. Mirel and Karen Bonnel Werth, *Stepping Stones to Jewish Spiritual Living* (Woodstock, Vt.: Jewish Lights Publishing, 1998), 6-11.

2. Gwen Shamblin, *The Weigh Down Diet* (New York: Doubleday, 1997), 1, 2.

3. Mary Pipher, *Reviving Ophelia: Saving the Lives of Adolescent Girls* (New York: Ballantine Books, 1994).

4. C. S. Lewis, *Perelandra* (New York: Macmillan, 1944), 217.

5. Esther de Waal, *The Celtic Way of Prayer: The Recovery of the Religious Imagination* (New York: Doubleday, 1997).

6. Gail Sheehy, *Understanding Men's Passages* (New York: Random House, 1998).

Chapter 5

1. Robert Bly, "The Long Bag We Drag Behind Us," *Meeting the Shadow: The Hidden Power of the Dark Side of Human Nature*, ed. Connie Zweig and Jeremiah Abrams (New York: Putnam and Sons, 1991), 6.

2. Janice Brewi and Anne Brennan, "Emergence of the Shadow in Midlife," in Zweig and Abrams, eds. *Meeting the Shadow,* 261.

3. Carol Tavris, *Anger: The Misunderstood Emotion* (New York: Simon and Schuster, 1982).

4. William A. Miller, "Finding the Shadow in Daily Life," in Zweig and Abrams, eds. *Meeting the Shadow*, 43. Much of the material in this section on observing the emergence of the shadow comes from this essay by William Miller.

5. Miller, "Finding the Shadow," 43-44.

Chapter 7

1. I have used a name for each of the eight patterns of spirituality in this chapter, such as "Energizer" here. Each name describes people for whom one of these functions is dominant. These eight names come from Reginald Johnson, *Your Spirituality and God* (Wheaton, Ill.: Victor Books, 1988). This book was formerly entitled *Celebrate My Soul.*

Chapter 8

1. Kenneth Alan Moe, *The Pastor's Survival Manual* (Bethesda, Md.: The Alban Institute, 1995), 43, 44.

2. Roy M. Oswald, *Clergy Self-Care: Finding a Balance for Effective Ministry* (Washington D.C.: The Alban Institute: 1991), x.

3. These statements about conflict come from the Lombard Mennonite Peace Center's course, "Conflict Resolution Skills for Churches," taught by Bob Williamson.

4. Oswald, *Clergy Self-Care*, 95.

5. Anthony G. Pappas, *Pastoral Stress: Sources of Tension, Resources for Transformation* (Bethesda, Md.: The Alban Institute, 1995), 26.

6. The Center for Career Development in Ministry is one of 12 ecumenical centers around the country that provide vocational development and psychological assessment for people preparing for ministry, for clergy seeking to clarify their call or direction, and for lay people who want to explore career options. They all offer a variety of programs that can be tailored to individual needs. If you would like to get the name and address of a center near you, write or call the Center for Career Development in Ministry, 70 Chase Street, Newton Center, MA, 02459, 617-969-7750.

7. Pappas, *Pastoral Stress*, 59, 60. Pappas has taken these 10 models from Margaret Fletcher Clark's article "Ten Models of Ordained Ministry" in *Action Information* IX, no. 5 (November-December 1983).